WINNING BODY LANGUAGE

LANGUAGE

FOR

SALES

PROFESSIONALS

WINNING BODY LANGUAGE

FOR

SALES

PROFESSIONALS

CONTROL THE CONVERSATION
AND CONNECT WITH YOUR CUSTOMER
—WITHOUT SAYING A WORD

MARK BOWDEN

WITH ANDREW FORD

New York   Chicago   San Francisco   Lisbon   London   Madrid   Mexico City
Milan   New Delhi   San Juan   Seoul   Singapore   Sydney   Toronto

1 2 3 4 5 6 7 8 9 0   QFR/QFR   1 8 7 6 5 4 3 2

ISBN   978-0-07-179300-1
MHID   0-07-179300-3

e-ISBN   978-0-07-179301-8
e-MHID   0-07-179301-1

Library of Congress Cataloging-in-Publication Data
Bowden, Mark.
    Winning body language for sales professionals : control the conversation and connect with your customer—without saying a word / by Mark Bowden.
        p. cm.
    ISBN-13: 978-0-07-179300-1 (alk. paper)
    ISBN-10: 0-07-179300-3 (alk. paper)
    1. Selling—Psychological aspects. 2. Body language. I. Title.
    HF5438.8.P75B69 2013
    658.8501'9—dc23

                                                                    2012027292

The following terms are trademarks of TruthPlane™ Inc.: GesturePlane™, TruthPlane™, PassionPlane™, GrotesquePlane™, DisclosurePlane™, DoorPlane™, TablePlane™, YesState™, PentaPoint™, and Rapid Resonance™.

To Tracey for always making the impossible possible.
—Mark Bowden

To my wife, Diane, and my mother, Jessica, in appreciation
of their unwavering support for everything I do.
—Andrew Ford

Contents

Preface

I first met Mark Bowden in March 2008. I was introduced to him via two associates who had "just met this great public speaking coach and body language expert!" and thought I should meet him too. Both Mark and I were based out of Toronto, and so, curious, we arranged to meet over coffee.

You might be wondering why I say "curious." I was already a very accomplished public speaker and seminar leader in the world of sales performance management. My ratings were always top of the top. I had a loyal following of fans and workshop attendees across North America and beyond. Yet two of my best supporters were adamant that I meet with this communication coach. You can imagine that something started nagging at me as to why exactly they were being so insistent.

Now, prior to venturing into my profession as a consultant—launching Sales CoPilot in 2006—I had been (not to blow my own trumpet—but I will) a pretty successful salesperson, sales manager, and even scaled the heights to be president of a division in an enterprise software company. Great communication had gotten me some distance professionally, and it would have been fair to rate me as an above-average presenter. Indeed, some would have said a pretty damned solid—even "expert"—communicator. But don't take my word for it: as a young man and at my mother's encouragement, I had joined Toastmasters and successfully completed my 10-speech curriculum, to achieve what was called at the time the

Competent Toastmaster certificate. Ask my mother and she'll dig it out to show you! So, through upbringing, training, and extensive professional experience, I was no wilting flower—comfortable with myself and comfortable in front of others, whether one-on-one with the CEO of a multinational, speaking before a packed convention, or in front of a couple of dozen industry specialists hammering me for solutions. Then why should I need a communication coach, even "one of the great ones"?

When I sat down for coffee that day, it was with an air of (probably healthy) skepticism as well as an unusual edge of negativity. You've seen it from the other side of the table, no doubt. Everything about your prospects, the way they sit, speak, and look at you when you talk says, "Okay, prove it!"

Then Mark calmly and confidently walked in, shook my hand and smiled, sat down next to me, and asked me some questions . . . and everything changed.

It was one of those pivotal meetings that we all find periodically in our careers. The influential impact of Mark's immediate insights and subtle coaching (there and then—in Starbucks) quickly extended past my presentation skills and into more general professional sales communication, and beyond! But I will begin here in the arena of presenting.

As a speaker I am a high-energy guy. I bring truckloads of enthusiasm and a freight train of passion to my work. I am absorbed by and immersed in the world of sales, and so I have amassed a wealth of domain expertise in system and process design, messaging, management, and coaching. When facing a group, I draw on this knowledge with warmth and enthusiasm. I am gregarious and put myself out there—you have to, to win attention and respect. If you don't give heart and soul, then your clients won't either.

When I present, I constantly strive for an interactive environment. Just like in any sales communication, seminars work best if the content is driven by the client's needs and you travel together toward shared insights. So it was in that meeting over coffee with Mark, as he gently questioned me about my communication style and I responded, that I had a shocking insight: *my passionate energy, in great part manifested through my body language, was creating a serious risk to my bigger business objectives.* So much so that at times I was overwhelming my audience and thus suppressing the interactive, conversational engagement that both they and I valued so highly.

I hired Mark on the spot to coach me going forward—now how's that for *his* sales ability? This took two forms: Mark reviewed some videos of past seminars I had facilitated. He then had me "present" to him, and we videotaped those sessions.

During our time together, Mark introduced me to his unique GesturePlane™ system, something you will learn more about in this book but at the time was not yet published and became available to the wider public through his first book, *Winning Body Language.* The only way to get Mark's groundbreaking training then was face-to-face, and so at a high price financially. Today you can quickly learn exactly what I learned back then by simply reading this book and trying out the nonverbal and psychological techniques in Mark's unique GesturePlane system. As he taught me: the mind and the body are interconnected—how the mind feels, the body in some way echoes or resonates. Yet Mark's GesturePlane system is unique in its understanding of how to more extensively utilize the extraordinary personal and social power of this connection—in reverse!

What your body displays—the minds of both you and your audience echo.

In my case, my customary public speaking body language was working *against* my intention of inviting interaction and collaboration. And as Mark quickly predicted, it was also wearing me out and interfering with my ability to be fully present to my audience, especially when it came to listening. Not to jump too far ahead, but Mark Bowden's GesturePlane system breaks the body up into horizontal gestural sections that align with some predictable feelings, judgments, and an élan—the quality of energy—an audience will inhabit when you use them. Whether you need your audience to empathize with the open and honest effect of the TruthPlane™, or the high energy of the PassionPlane™, or kept away from the low energy and disinterest brought on by the GrotesquePlane™: put your gestures at the appropriate horizontal level, and your emotion, attitude, and energy will follow that lead. In short: engage yourself in the corresponding body language to the engagement you want from your clients and customers. Be the change you want to see.

I was in the PassionPlane way too much: overpowering my audience or exhausting them. This not only interfered with their taste and stamina for interaction but also inhibited my own ability to listen to subtle feedback as I focused on pushing out a kilowatt performance every time. Not the best combination for a customer-centric sales conversation.

Don't get me wrong—just like you now, I was still a very, very good communicator, successful with my current audience and clients. But like hypertension in a 40-year-old, the damage is hard to see at first, yet cumulative. Looking back, I can see numerous instances where my posture and power either inhibited my audience from sharing fully and freely or inspired me to jump on a "dissenting opinion" way before I knew its true colors. To further disclose the true colors of my personality profile: when I describe myself as high energy, I'm not kidding. In one personality test, the Hogan Assessments of Personality Inventory, I scored super high on energy. The prize: I am an enthusiastic and passionate leader. The punishment: under pressure, or when tired, this energy can bubble over into aggression and be disruptive. In leadership coaching, the coach would focus on helping a leader with my profile to manage this energy level in order to reduce the risk of intimidating members of the team.

Working with Mark, I saw this balancing act with greater clarity. Through TruthPlane, he gave me the key to achieving the right balance—not through the way I thought, but the way I moved.

The GesturePlane system gave me a new insight and new controls. The difference in my work was noticeable and measurable. Mark had a great description of the difference in those early days that is worth repeating: "At the end of your presentation, did the audience respect your content, or did they respect your content and want to go for a coffee to spend more time with *you*." Before working with Mark, I was earning great respect for my content but spending too much time afterward alone over coffee when I would have been better served enjoying my latte with a lineup of prospective clients, eager to converse more with *me*.

Now, not only am I better at engaging my audience to move further into productive sales conversations, but I better engage myself. My mind stays clearer; my focus is easier to maintain. I am more aware of the environment I'm creating and how I can influence it in support of my message. If I feel my energy rising and it serves no useful purpose to my goals, I can literally stem the flow on purpose. You see, the body is not just a reflection of the mind; the body can influence the mind. Left unattended, the body will follow and express or indicate in some way your emotional state; however, if you attend and maintain awareness of your body, it will influence your feelings, attitude, and energy. This is the magic of Mark's research and practice.

One of the insights I offered to Mark after our work together was that I found the greatest impact in my one-on-one communication. In my personal interactions when coaching salespeople, entrepreneurs, or selling to a customer, my energy issue was of course just as prevalent as it was in speaking. I ran the risk of my energy level overwhelming the listener and interfering with the interactive intent of the message. In worst case scenarios it could actually be intimidating. After working with Mark, I had a new tool that allowed me to turn the volume down when needed.

Now when I want someone to interact, share, be engaged, I can use my body language to create an environment and atmosphere that invites the audience to enroll in the process. If faced with a low reacting, disinterested audience, I can use my body language to help draw them out and share with me in spite of themselves. It is not manipulation—it is about using the most fundamental social instincts developed through thousands of years of human evolution, and before that several million years of continuity between species—the instinctual behavior we inherit from deep in our DNA.

Mark's focus has traditionally been with leaders and speakers trying to inspire audiences with just the right impact. But his work at its core is about ensuring that you create the *environment* for any communication to be most effective. It is this element in particular that brought me to collaborate with him on *Winning Body Language for Sales Professionals*. A sale, at its best, is a collaborative effort with the customers to find the right answer for them. The best salespeople are greater listeners than they are talkers. They build strong interpersonal trusting relationships. Learning to manage your body language to support the creation of this atmosphere, whether meeting a consumer on the floor of a retail store or trying to convince the CEO of a large corporation that you can help him sleep better at night, is an opportunity to separate you from those who let their emotions run riot with their message.

In this book we will be walking you personally through Mark's unique principles of body language, nonverbal communication, and behavior, based on his extensive explorations and expertise in the arts, evolutionary psychology, neural architecture, and embodied cognition. We will then apply those principles to the many scenarios you face as a salesperson and hear from some top experts, bringing their unique and powerful insights from a diverse set of experiences. All this to help you create environments that maximize your chance for success and give you *Winning Body Language for Sales Professionals*.

Whether you are an established sales professional from any walk looking to get the edge on your competition and step up your game to the next level, or a young rookie looking to hit the ground at a rate that others just won't know exists—then we welcome you.

Andrew Ford
SalesCoPilot.com

Acknowledgments

First, thanks to Andrew Ford for joining in with me on this book and working hard to make it so unique.

Thanks to everyone who originally made *Winning Body Language* such a huge and ongoing success, many of whom are the family, friends, colleagues, and contemporaries that I love and respect and who agreed to be guest contributors: Shaun Prendergast, Bruce Van Ryn-Bocking, Michael Bungay Stanier, Jennifer La Trobe, Michael Leckie, Niki Winterson, Jack Milner, Ivor Benjamin, Leah Morrigan, Farrell Macdonald, Paul Nazareth, Tamara Glick, Annie Izmirliyan, Jeremy Miller, Rona Birenbaum, James Lavers, Janine Harris, Karen Wright, and of course my wife Tracey Thomson, without whom this book would be totally sad and unreadable, and like life without her, would really never happen at any enjoyable, interesting, or sustainable level. You are amazing!

Lex and Stella, thank you for coming over and giving me kisses when I was working on this.

Mum, Dad, Ann, Helen, and David, I am always thinking of you.

Thank you to all of my clients and colleagues who have pushed forward a fuller understanding of the power of nonverbal communication for business, leadership, and sales with me, and continue to support my work.

And finally, thanks to my agent and publishers: Carolyn Forde and Bruce Westwood at Westwood Creative Artists, and Donya Dickerson at McGraw-Hill.

Mark Bowden

I would like to thank Mark for inviting me to participate in this project. His support and confidence in me and my contribution have been overwhelming. It has been a pleasure to have such a partner on my first book-writing project.

Thanks to Tracey Thomson for her resourceful support to both Mark and me in completing this book.

I would also like to mention all the support and experiences I have enjoyed with my colleagues, mentors, salespeople, and customers who helped me form the understanding of sales that enables both my consulting practice and contributions to this project. There are too many great people to mention them all in this short note, but I would like to make special mention of my colleagues Marie Wiese, Colin Marcelline, Joel Lessem, and Jeff Austin. Each of them has helped me move my thinking forward. Another special mention goes to the many regular participants in the YTA Sales Peer group I facilitate, which creates a forum to test new and innovative sales ideas. Brenda Dryall also deserves a special mention for her support of my sales research over the years. She has put up with highlighted books, poor dictation recordings, and aggressive timelines with never a complaint.

Finally, but most important, I would like to thank my wife, Diane, for her unwavering support and positive reinforcement in everything I do.

Andrew Ford

Introduction

As you pick up this book to start reading, the question is—why would body language be so important to sales? Either you have already answered that question for yourself, bought this book, and are now well on your way to discovering powerful new nonverbal tips, tricks, and techniques that will help any sales professionals to build trust and credibility with their customers and clients; or you need that question answered for you before you commit to buying your own copy of *Winning Body Language for Sales Professionals* right now.

Of course, a third possibility is that you do not believe that having a better understanding of nonverbal communication could have any significant impact whatsoever on a sales process for you, and you are reading this introduction in spite of yourself. Good, you'll like the next paragraph.

You are right—there are theorists on sales who insist that people simply buy any product or service in order to fulfill a technical need. They say that buyers wish to move away from a "pain" they are experiencing, and everything about the alleviation of that "pain" can be dealt with by getting exactly the right features wrapped into a product or service. When you as the salesperson can do that for them, they buy. So there is no need for any of this "soft skill" body language hokum when you sell. Competitive advantage comes down to how well you make your offering fit the niche of the problem. Only technical cataloging is needed to represent a product or service to a new or existing customer. The catalog will clearly state the "gap" the customer or client is experiencing and link that gap to a product or service that fills the need. This catalog could be printed (expensive), online (cheap), or human (very expensive). But all it needs to do is accurately communicate a fit between the product or service and the gap, and *bingo*—they buy.

If you did not nod your head at least partially in agreement with that last statement, then please put this book down (it does not belong to you—and if it does, go and get your money back from the retailer; you've made a serious error). Get yourself over to the "Fantasy" section of the bookstore—you'll like it better over there.

Right, that got them out of the way.

The combination of "Field of Dreams" theory and "build a better mousetrap" strategy in the real world has caused thousands of inventive products and services to gather dust; to be lonely, forgotten, and abandoned in the dark basements, bright imaginations, and crushed dreams of their creators. Because most stuff simply can't sell itself.

Clients and customers have to *trust* before they can buy. It comes down to the sales professional to help build the trust and credibility that engages a client or customer. Great salespeople build trust, credibility, and engagement faster and more easily than average salespeople. Their behaviors differentiate them from the crowd, enroll their prospects in the sales process, and lead everyone to the most successful outcomes.

We buy from the people we trust, and we keep on buying from people we keep on trusting. We buy from credible people, and we make referrals to those we find trustworthy and credible. We hang out with people who engage us, and we see them as leaders. Yet, how do we actually *know* whether to trust anyone as a credible leader or not?

If people were buying from you, how would they know instantly that you were a person they could trust to keep their best interests at heart? What mechanism and process would they utilize to instantly and accurately judge your credibility, and so comfortably decide there and then to engage with you to lead them along the sales path—and maybe also even take the greatest risk of bringing others in their team along for the ride?

For many hundreds of thousands of years we Homo sapiens, like our 2.5 million year old ancestors from the Homo genus, along with many other animal organisms across our planet have survived and thrived by unconsciously judging the *physical behavior* of others in order to quickly work out whether another entity's actions are "safe" or "suspect"—if they are "friend" or "enemy"—and to what degree that prediction can be trusted over time; that is, is it credible and thus worthy of confidence and further investment. The ability to use complex verbal language is very new to humans (approximately 100,000 years old), and so we still instinctively rely on taking in each other's nonverbal behavior in order to discern the intention or feeling another human being has for us. By judging others' body language, we quickly decide if we can walk along a path with them, if we should back out right now, or if we should force them out of our territory immediately.

And so it is with sales: the prospects decide if they should take the sales journey prescribed by you, or invite you to join them on their prescribed path, or see you out of their space before you've even opened your mouth to say, "Can I help you?" or "What are the most pressing business issues for you, today?" They decide quickly, instinctively, and quite often irrevocably, and they decide based on nonverbal behavior.

Now let's not get this wrong—what you say to a prospective customer or client with your verbal language is always of great, great importance. It is the icing on the cake. But if there is no cake, then often all we are left with is a sticky mess: a saccharine, unwholesome experience with no long-lasting feelings of benefit. It is this lack of a solid foundation that gets us into the territory of "snake oil"—when the "miracle cure" that was promised verbally from the back of a buckboard wagon turns out to be a rancorous disappointment when we get home.

The "cake" for any sales professional has to be your body language, your nonverbal communication, your behavior during the sales process. Get this layer of behavior right, and people trust you instantly, feel they can trust what you say, and then attach those feelings of trust and confidence to being in your company, your organization, your brand, and of course ultimately have trust and confidence in what you have to sell to them.

So the reason this book is important to you is that ultimately *people buy feelings, not things*. Remember that. In fact, let's say it again and underline it to emphasize just how important understanding this is to your increased sales success from today onward: People buy feelings, not things. Every step customers take along the sales path—every interaction they experience— gives them feelings, and that is part of how your product or service is judged. Everyone who is (or is not) a buyer for you subconsciously keeps a mental checklist of positive and negative feelings and adjusts the score as he goes. Feelings such as safety, belonging, confusion, clarity, and prestige will certainly have contributed to the tally before you have even introduced the technical features of what is on offer to the buyer.

Now once again, it is always totally understandable to be thinking, "You know what . . . my product is so awesome that I can overcome all those petty feelings that potential customers have!" And once again some of you (who should have put down this book a few paragraphs back and started rereading *The Lord of the Rings*) may be right: a really good product that provides an overwhelmingly positive feeling, or leads to many positive feelings, can overcome almost anything. But this is rare at best and most usually a fantasy.

Here's some reality. This book can help you to personally construct a sales experience that in a significant and sustainable way increases the neurochemistry responsible for the good feelings and the human connection that ultimately helps buyers feel they have done the right thing, made the right choice, made their life more stable and predictable, and that they are holding a valuable resource that has a high status in their social group.

And this is the case whether it is a complex business-to-business sale or the most simple—but no less important—business-to-consumer transaction.

This training will help you create the right environment to host the deep experience any buyer is looking for. Because (although ordinarily any Request for Proposal will omit this point, and customers generally will not utter it as they walk into your place of business), as any medical doctor knows, *the presenting problem is not the real problem*. The initial "painful" symptom that motivates any of us toward a sales consultation can in some cases be the result of a haphazard or Band-Aid solution we have executed in order to quickly deal with or perhaps even ignore the *real* underlying issues that we *should* actually be addressing.

Whatever the case, there is greater meaning attached to everything we buy. And it can be the job of the highest performing sales professionals to help their customers and clients define and understand that meaning; to take customers on an exploration of that meaning and have the buyers feel truly comfortable with the direction they eventually take alongside them. That sales professional has to use *influence* (to get "inflow" with the clients, empathize with their current course—accept their feelings) and eventually *persuasion* (to move them hard). This is in essence a structure for helping other human beings with a behavioral change, and in the case of sales, for moving them from nonpurchasers to purchasers.

To move them along on this journey in a faster, more comfortable, and powerful way, this book is going to help move you through mastery of your nonverbal communication so that you can consciously control and adapt the environment around the person, your client, whose behavior you wish to change. Once again, it is important to note how words are still important here. No doubt there are some amazing things you can do with words to influence and persuade others into some dynamic changes in behavior. Yet, if given the choice of changing the environment around the trickiest prospective customers in order to change their behavior *versus* talking them into a change, many experts in influence would take the former as having the greatest leverage when it really matters most. Why? Because language is highly, highly complex; whereas movement, though full of complexities as well, remains a vastly simpler communication channel by which to consciously influence the unconscious mind and, importantly, the behavior it governs, toward some very predictable outcomes.

Let's look at an example from the animal world.

Imagine an ant—a social insect with a very simple mechanical and neural system, which causes it to make its way to food and other resources the individual ant and its colony need to survive. Now, place your ant at one end of a flat, white surface, and place a food source for the ant at the other end. You will find, perhaps unsurprisingly, that the ant takes a very quick and direct journey toward the goal—the food source—it is instinctively designed to go for. Now take your imaginary ant and place it at one end of the exact same square footage of a sandy beach with its food placed the same distance away again. What do you imagine happens now? Well, if you do this with a real ant, its trajectory toward the goal will show a lot of twists, turns, about-faces, back-peddling, missing-it-by-a-mile, and general "noodling around" types of behavior: irregular, unpredictable, downright complicated, and mind-bogglingly inefficient.

Without seeing how easy it was for your ant to get what it wanted the first time around, this second experiment could lead you to suppose that ants have some very complicated behaviors around searching for food, or as a group are not very bright; or just that "we got a dud'un 'ere!" But with the knowledge of both instances, it turns out that the complexity of the behavior is a response to the complexity of the environment. The ant itself is using a set of very simple rules to move it toward its goal. In this ant, it is the interaction of these rules with the environment that actually produces something akin to moving a "tricky customer" to see the solution.

So shall we *speak* to the ant about how it could better move through the environment or see if we can swap the sandy beach for something a little easier for the ant to navigate?

This is not such a facetious a question as it might at first seem. The ant, like us, has a gene for language switched on. It can communicate through the emission of pheromones—chemicals that trigger a social response in members of the same species—exactly what it predicts the *future* may hold for others at a distant location. This ability for what communication experts call "displacement"—being able to refer to objects, places, and events that are "not here" and "not now"—is one of the factors that can categorize an organism as possessing "language." So if you were to learn or become enabled with the ant's language, you could signal to it the best path to take for its future success. Yet you can see how this is all going to pan out: while you are busy trying to code the best way to get your message across to the ant, it has of course walked off in the opposite direction. By the time you've really honed your message, the ant has moved on as a worker to an ant farm in your competitor's territory— or so you hear.

So rather than learning the ant's unique language and laying down a complex set of instructions for it, and knowing that it is the ant's *environment* that is causing unhelpful behaviors—some would much prefer to place it within a simpler environment for it to achieve the goal, if they could.

This is what *Winning Body Language for Sales Professionals* is all about. In order to change the behavior of your current prospects and clients, we are going to work on changing the environment around them. We are going to control the nonverbal communication environment around ourselves and others in order to help both us and them hit the targets desired. By using clear and simple behavior, we will influence and persuade clients and customers toward the feelings that imbue the goal of buying from you with a meaning that is resonant for them and that they *really* want.

You are going to learn how to change your own physical environment— your own body language and nonverbal communication during any sales process—in order to control your own behavior and to influence the feelings and meaning that the sales process has for you and everyone around you: partners, team, clients, and customers. You will learn how to *control the conversation, connect with your customer, and close the sale—without saying a word*. And ultimately by reading this book and following its tips, tricks, and techniques, you and your customers will feel more satisfied with the sales experience than ever before. So read on and be prepared to move both your customer and *yourself* to the next level.

A-B-C. A-Always, B-Be, C-Closing. Always be closing, always be closing.

—Blake, *Glengarry Glen Ross*, David Mamet

1

Primary Impressions

Getting Past "Indifference"

There is continuity between species ... Man with all his noble qualities
still bears in his bodily frame the indelible stamp of his lowly origin.
— Charles Darwin

In this chapter you'll learn:

- The important science around nonverbal communication
- Exactly how your primitive brain sees others
- The pitfalls of the primal snap judgments others make about you
- The most important first impressions to give — and to avoid
- More powerful roles to play in the sales process

If legend is to be believed, prostitution is the world's oldest profession. In other words, it could stand to reason that selling sex is the oldest sales profession we have. However, back in the days of prehistory there were other essentials to our human survival potentially just as important as sex and reproduction, such as: food, heat, shelter, and safety. All of these, including sex, could be used as currency and exchanged for whichever of the others was lacking for survival. But of course any one of these became valuable only when in short supply.

If we presume that our early ancestors were either more promiscuous or perhaps a less sexually repressed society than today's, we can expect there may have been no supply issues to a mutually high demand for sexual activity in prehistoric times. And so, back then there might have been no real reason anyone needed to convince, persuade, negotiate, or influence anyone else into sex! Some psychologists suggest, then, that prostitution in fact evolved not from the selling of sex, but from the selling of sex with limited attachment or responsibility. If this theory is correct, the oldest sales profession is not the selling of tangible sex but of an intangible *future* in which, after the sexual act, there would be "no strings attached."

Why is all of this being brought to your attention? Well, some say sex sells. And so the hope is that it has hooked you into reading this chapter a little farther.

Value Propositioning

In theory, selling is at its core simply this: offering to exchange something for something else. The something of value being offered may be tangible or intangible, real or conceptual. Both the *something* and the *something else* are most often seen by the seller and the buyer as of value. And it is implied that the process between the buyer and seller will proceed fairly and ethically so that both parties end up rewarded.

This kind of transaction has been happening from the very first day a group of humans found themselves hungry and short of fuel to cook an antelope they found dead and decaying on the dry African savannah. They may have looked over at a neighboring family with a stack of wood and signaled to them in an effort to determine if they would be interested in "going halves" on some safe *roast* meat in exchange for the fuel to cook it with.

Trusting in the Sale

As long as there is a tangible demand and a tangible supply, with something tangible to exchange that is equally or more valued, there is potentially an easy exchange to be had. But if there are indeterminate factors to the exchange, which cannot be immediately sensed and so are *intangible* or conceptual, then the buyer and/or the seller have to go on *trust* that the correct order of events will occur to ensure that the agreed upon set of circumstances will prevail to satisfy the transaction for both parties.

Ultimately, both parties shake hands and trust that the deal will culminate in the exchange of something real. However, in any exchange like this there are often looming questions: Will there be the supply or payment asked for and expected? Will it happen in the time span agreed upon? Will the concept discussed work in reality? Will it keep on working? If it stops working, what will the after-sales service be like? Will the supply be used in an incorrect manner by the buyer, causing him to abuse the after-sales service?

Of course, all of these factors and many, many more exist in the future and can be talked about verbally by the parties involved in the transaction; but what you are going to be finding and facing over the course of this book is that the "talk" around these intangible futures is often not enough to gain those initial levels of trust needed to *start,* or for that matter maintain, any profitable, long-term sales relationship.

And That's a Guarantee

Predictability is a key to trust: if we have seen that what you say turns out to be true once, twice, maybe three times, then we can start to predict that you walk your talk and do what you say you will do. However, if we have never done business with you before, then what is the mechanism for us to know that we can predict you are trustworthy? What needs to happen so we don't have to take some kind of blind "leap of faith" and risk being disappointed and out of pocket if "faith" turns out to be ill placed in you?

"Trust Me—I'm in Sales!"

We use nonverbal communication, including body language, as one of our major data sources to make what are inevitably long-lasting snap judgments about whether we can really trust someone or not. We all do it— and we always have done it. And as you will be finding out, even with technological advances in modern communication, we are still reliant on nonverbal communication as a primary source of raw data for creating our *feelings* about whether we are making the right decisions when we buy.

What does science tell us about how much we rely on nonverbal communication in deciding whether we can trust someone?

If we extrapolate from the famous studies of Albert Mehrabian, professor emeritus of psychology, UCLA (*Decoding of Inconsistent Communications* and *Inference of Attitudes from Nonverbal Communication in Two Channels,* 1967), it certainly appears that the nonverbal elements of human communication are particularly important in transmitting information that influences and forms the receiver's understanding of the *emotion, attitude,* or *intent* behind the message being communicated. Indeed, this is true to such an extent that it is suggested that body language accounts for 55 percent of that data, tone of voice accounts for 38 percent, and the verbal content (i.e., the words) supplies 7 percent of the data used by the receiver to gain an overall *feeling* of the attitude, intent, or emotion behind what someone is communicating. This implies in turn that the emotion, attitude, or intent that others *feel* we are communicating is likely to be more heavily linked to our nonverbal message than our verbal one.

If the Clothes Fit . . .

With all this in mind, try this on for size: Imagine you are selecting an item of clothing from a store. You take a few pieces to the changing room and come back out a few minutes later wearing one of them in order to check out the look in the store's full-length mirror. You turn to the sales assistant and say, "How does this look on me?" You notice his nose wrinkles slightly, the corners of his lips go down, and his lower lip depresses — a reaction of *disgust* is on his face. Will you be buying this piece of clothing now? Possibly not? Let's go back in and try on a different piece, and while you are changing, think about the following:

Dr. Mehrabian's findings have led the majority of communication experts to conclude that to produce effective messages, the words, sound, and body need to support one another. They must be *congruent*. In the case of any incongruity, the receiver of the message will trust the predominant *nonverbal* cues rather than the potential literal meaning of the words.

Out you come again from the changing room wearing a second piece. You take a look in the mirror again and then turn and ask the sales assistant, "How does this one look on me?"

"Fantastic!" he replies, which *sounds* very promising, but once again you see that same look of disgust, and on top of all this he is now shaking his head rapidly from side to side and with a hard swallowing motion in the throat and also scrunching up around his eyes.

You may never shop here again, because the staff members are not all that adept at offering positive help; however, it is fair to say they make it abundantly clear (nonverbally) how they feel about *your* choices.

What is the point of all this getting dressed and undressed? Well, given this second insight from Dr. Mehrabian's research, it is fair to say that in general we humans *need to see it to believe it*! So how did this continuing reliance on nonverbal communication to establish and sustain trust come about? Let's go further back in history to before humans had the ability to communicate verbally to when our nearest ancestors first made an impression on the planet.

Facts Are Rare

We are going to take a scientific view on exactly why we human beings communicate in the way we do today. First, a quick discussion about science.

Is science true, and the only *real* story? There are no guarantees; and science is certainly not meant to be a faith. With science, a "fact" that seemed true and certain yesterday may tomorrow become uncertain; and yet it may become possible again the day after that. The scientific community can often then rethink, reexamine, reevaluate, and find that the "facts" were misguided, misjudged, or misinformed.

Can't science make up its mind? In many areas of scientific study, new data and knowledge are coming in all the time. These can change (and hopefully improve) scientific theories and the way they are tested, along with the experiments and instruments used to test them. Science has been constantly changing our view of reality, and those who are scientifically minded or practiced have to ensure that the scientific theories fit the scientific picture, and vice versa. Science can in some ways be seen as *the best idea we have today based on how we went looking for that idea.* And it is on this scientific basis that the stories and ideas around evolution, biology, and human communication you are about to read arrive to you.

Out of Africa

Today, all humans belong to one population of Homo sapiens, undivided by species barrier. However, according to what is known by many as the "Out of Africa" model, this is not the first species of hominids: the first species of the genus Homo, known as *Homo habilis*, evolved in East Africa at least 2 million years ago, and members of this species spread to many different areas of the African continent. A little later (1.8 million years back), *Homo erectus* evolved, and by 1.5 million years back had spread across the world as it looked then. This Out-of-Africa theory, supported now with research using female mitochondrial DNA and the male Y chromosome, says that modern Homo sapiens evolved in Africa 200,000 years ago, began migrating from Africa between 70,000 and 50,000 years ago, and eventually replaced the preexisting hominid species in Europe and Asia.

Our ancestors stretch back hundreds of thousands of years and more. And a good chunk of our behavior is inherited from the early humans who had no neural capacity (or need at the time) for spoken language, let alone the cultural ability to sustain it over generations. But of course, these earliest ancestors did have nonverbal communication. So what was its purpose?

Social Control

The primary purpose of nonverbal communication is to manipulate the actions of others in a social group *right now*—and not at a later date.

Nonverbal communication is designed therefore for *immediate effect*. The nonverbal communication that we are talking about here and throughout this book is not indexical or symbolic, that is, it is not a type of manual sign language, as for example when someone points at something and makes a barking "woof, woof" sound to say, "That thing over there I place in the category of *dog.*"

When we talk about body language in this book, we are referring to the most primitive of nonverbal communication designed to change the behavior of others immediately by signaling the emotion, attitude, or intent that you have for the situation *now*. For example, you may unconsciously throw a look of *contempt* (the corners of your lips tighten and rise on one side of the face) at your sales partner, who (alongside you on an important face-to-face sales call) points at the framed picture of a person on your prospective customer's desk and makes a "woof, woof" sound. A nonverbal facial gesture of contempt such as this is just one of many primitive social signals designed to communicate *immediately* to another in your group that they have broken a social rule designed for the survival or "fitness" of all—in this case the sales team and your company as a whole—and in doing so the communicator runs the risk of exclusion from the group. In this example, it is the unspoken social rule of "do not offend the potential customer by suggesting they have a family member who resembles a dog."

The Archimedes Principle

So body "language" is not, strictly speaking, a "language" at all, if we understand that one of the deciding characteristics for language is its ability to *displace*—displacement in communication is the ability to represent events or concepts that occur in the past or the future. Languages can be used to communicate ideas about things that are not in the immediate vicinity either spatially or temporally, or both. Our primitive nonverbal language does not have the capability to do this.

For example, there is no physical way, except for the use of complex sign language, signal, index, symbol, or other representation, to communicate to another human being: "How about I drop by with a sample of my new product *next week*, when I hope you'll be over your quite understandable anger at my sales partner's abject rudeness; perhaps then you will be better able to see how our company's product fits your company's five-year growth plan that we've been discussing together over the last six months. Meanwhile, I'm now going back to the office in order to convince our sales manager to fire this joker next to me for single-handedly jeopardizing months of work with this inappropriate attempt at some kind of comic mime!" You can, however, display your sincere and continued good feelings *now* toward your prospective customer by saying those words while smiling warmly; and you certainly will communicate your current negative feelings and intentions toward your coworker *now* by the flash of anger in your look toward them. Nonverbal communication is powerful and economical, and the right nonverbal signals *now* could mean the difference between saving the client or losing the client forever.

It is nonverbal communication, with its rapid fire of emotional, intentional, and attitudinal data, that causes others to quickly and most fully comply and change their behavior in often a fraction of a second. This economy in the use of nonverbal communication is its power and advantage over much of our verbal language.

Dr. Dolittle

Nonverbal communication in human beings is fundamentally an "animal communication system." In other words, human nonverbal communication conveys information between us that relates to basic individual survival, mating, and social needs. Some communications are hard to fit into a single one of these categories.

For example, a nonverbal signal of appeasement, used in confrontations when your enemy looks to be winning, is a social signal *and* a survival signal—if you don't make it, you could get hurt. But it might be fair to say that no nonverbal signal falls outside of these categories: no animal communication signal or nonverbal signal can be used to communicate exclusively about the weather, the scenery, or your neighbor's latest drama—though a signal can communicate your attitude, emotion, and intention with regard to how you are situated for survival, mating, or social positioning within those environments. What is most important for an understanding of the limits of nonverbal communication as this book defines and examines it is that it certainly cannot communicate the future plans or past experiences of all these things.

Lazy Speech

Why, before the evolution of human language, did humans not have the ability to displace and therefore reminisce about past events, or plan and coopt others into often quite conceptual activities around the future? The simple answer is that *evolution is minimalist*. Any organism will do only the very least to fit into and exploit its ecological niche. Our ancestors required only nonverbal Animal Communication Systems (ACS) to survive, and so language did not develop until it was necessary for our survival as a species. Once the environment around early humans changed so that displacement became an advantage, any subtle movement toward the capacity for language was "fitter," and so survived, and that capacity was then passed on through the genes to the next generations.

We are designed to adapt when it is of benefit to our survival through the process of natural selection; beyond this, the brain and the body do nothing more than they have to. We are limited by what we have to work with, that is, the bodily shapes and mental abilities at any given moment, and the behavior that this architecture and its qualities make possible within the environment.

Darwin said that adaptability, and not intelligence or strength, is ultimately the key to a species' survival, even if it means evolving into a new species better adapted to thrive under new conditions. Humans developed language as our surrounding conditions changed; the extra energy needed by a large neocortex to produce verbal language proved to be worth the cost, as opposed to facing the decline of our human species.

To understand more about this and why nonverbal communication is so powerful, let's take a quick look at the development and evolution of the brain. First: what do brains do?

Noggin

The brain takes information from the senses, analyzes that information, and translates it into commands that get sent back to the muscles. Remember, *evolution is lazy*, so brains don't do what they don't have to do, mainly because brains are energetically expensive. That's why some processes are looked after simply by the way the body interacts with the environment. For example, breathing out is passive; once you have breathed in, breathing out eventually happens as a result of air pressure. Similarly, when you walk, the downward motion of your foot is effectively enabled by gravity's effect on the mass of your whole body drawing it down toward the earth.

The next step of processing is done by the *archipallium* (primitive brain) or *brain stem* as some call it; this can be thought of as the *instinctual brain*, and some refer to it as the *reptilian brain*. Although the human brain uses about 20 percent of our entire energy, the part therein that is most essential to survival—the brain stem—uses only a fraction of this to, first, preserve the homeostasis, which it does by monitoring many conditions, both internal and external—anything from keeping our internal body temperature relatively constant within a narrow range to warning you when you are about to bump into something. But its range of behaviors more or less ends there: for example, it is not conscious of itself. It cannot make decisions about itself and then build new ideas about what course of action it should take. It operates only as a preprogrammed monitoring and response unit. It receives information about the environment from the senses and the body as a whole, and sends it to be analyzed for identification. Then, based on a threat analysis, it instantly executes a course of action.

But where does it get its method of analysis? How does it see the world? And upon what values does it judge it?

Talk to the Lizard

This reptilian brain is part and parcel of the *Reptilian Neural Complex*, or the *R-Complex* for short. This is a name given to the brain stem as described above, combined also with the structures of the medulla, pons, cerebellum, mesencephalon, basal ganglia, globus pallidus, the amygdala, and the olfactory bulbs (Figure 1.1). The term itself, with its reference to reptiles, is derived from the fact that comparative neuroanatomists (scientists who compare the anatomy of brains) find that the brains of reptiles (and birds) are composed almost exclusively from these simple structures. They find that this R-Complex is responsible for instinctual behaviors involved with aggression, dominance, territoriality, and ritual displays typical across a variety of species in the evolutionary chain from fish to us humans.

Remember that essentially *all models are wrong, but some are useful*. The useful thing about this model is to recognize that the system employed by our instinctual brain is inherited from ancestors stretching back farther than any Homo sapiens and back as far as 500 million years to a prereptilian state. In *On the Origin of Species*, Charles Darwin made two claims with particular relevance to this: that there is continuity of species, with each species today being descendants of prior ones; and that natural selec-

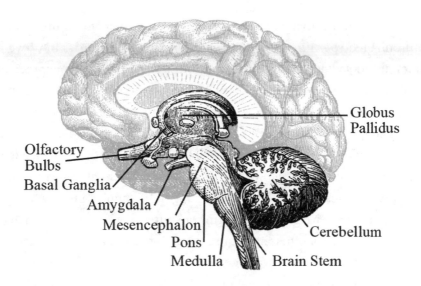

Globus
Pallidus

Olfactory
Bulbs

Basal Ganglia

Amygdala

Mesencephalon

Pons

Medulla

Cerebellum

Brain Stem

Figure 1.1 The Reptilian Brain

tion is the mechanism by which species change. In our DNA there is evidence that both of these statements are currently scientifically correct.

Just like our reptilian ancestors, the simple, instinctual brain gets first bite at all data. It gets to make unconscious snap judgments about that data in order to do the bare minimum to preserve life in our ecological niche. This aspect of the brain senses the immediate surroundings, and based on what it detects, quickly instructs the body to respond and react— some of these instinctual reactions are literally millions of years old. They are as such tried and tested, fail-safe responses to the stimuli.

Lazy Thinking

Nonverbal communication may provide some information that will reach your conscious mind, but that is merely a by-product. The primary function of your nonverbal communication is to get others to do things that will enhance *your* fitness. (If they enhance their own fitness too—well, that's just lucky for them!) Thus the impulse to "freeze" when a predator is detected at some distance is a "flight" gesture so the predator does not notice you and will expend its own energy furthering the distance between you by simply moving on. A simple unconscious action by one being can cause behaviors from the other that will render the situation to be fixed to the first's advantage. What need is there to fix a potential problem using your precious resources of critical thinking and complex physical action when an inexpensive gesture (in terms of your use of energy) can change the environment for others and cause them to react in a way that changes the situation to suit your own fitness?

With nonverbal communication that is designed to respond to tricky situations and manipulate other beings, you can see why the signals have to be bound to the "here and now." You can't respond to a situation in a distant time or space (at least you couldn't before the invention of communication technologies that could produce real-time communication over distance—though all such technologies, from fire and smoke signals to personal video communication, are still relatively young compared to our body and mind). Our nonverbal communication has developed, for most of its history, within an environment that dictates, "You can't manipulate somebody who isn't there yet." What may appear to be a limitation in nonverbal communication is born out of a basic survival necessity.

Categorically Moving

Nonverbal communication causes humans to unconsciously initiate preset strategies, or reactions, to the signal. It is not conceptual nor is it designed to elicit conceptual responses. A concept is something you can "think with." Nonverbal communication is designed to elicit a *categorical* response; in other words, we categorize the nonverbal signals coming at us, instinctively deciding how to order information — is that approaching shape a "tiger" or an "apple" or a "sales assistant"? Categorization allows for quick thinking when conceptualization could slow us down.

Looked through the lens of evolution, you might see how the brain's ability to make snap judgments best contributes to an animal's fitness: it decides what's out there, what dangers it faces, what opportunities await, and quickly instructs the rest of the body how to react. It's food — approach it! It's a predator — avoid it! It's healthy and of the same species — check if it's available to mate! It's moving but unidentified — freeze until further notice! Most of the time, of course, it's none of the above; no problem, go on doing whatever you're doing. What is important for this system is that the brain has to make a quick decision. So it divides things into categories that differ starkly from one another for quick classification . . . if it is def initely food, no way it can be a predator.

And so the four simple categories that our primitive, reptilian brains have for everything that makes up our environment including other humans can be best described as:

1. Friend
2. Enemy
3. Sex
4. Indifferent

Customer Survey

What does all this mean to the sales professional? Every time you meet your clients, their primitive and instinctual brain within a fraction of a second simply cannot help but put you into one of those four categories. Equally, your brain stem does the same with them. With more than 7 billion human beings on the planet Earth, the default category into which you are most likely to place others every time your reptilian brain meets someone is "indifferent"; and perhaps unsurprisingly, their reptilian brain is predisposed to place you in the "indifferent" category by default as well.

Why must "indifferent" be the default category? If we were predisposed to see everyone as "friend," we would not reach our individual goals because we would be so obsessed with socializing. A predisposition to see everyone as "friend" is contrary to our predisposition for survival and fitness: we would risk being stripped of all our resources by those few people who turned out to be predators and attacked before we could change our mind about them. Conversely, if we categorized everyone by default as our "enemy," we would be in an acute state of paranoia; never able to leave the house, that is if living in a house was even a viable option, as we would assume it had been built by an enemy and therefore totally unsafe! Finally, if we categorized by default everybody as "sexual partner" . . . well, you can imagine!

How does the brain make these classifications? Think of it like this: how do we know to approach an apple and avoid a tiger? How do we differentiate an apple as "friend" or resource from a tiger as "enemy" or predator? Do we need little packages of data in our heads, one labeled "apple," and the other "tiger"? Certainly not. A certain rhythm and pace of movement, or a combination of colors, can be used to alert us to something most likely in the predator or enemy category. The glimpse of a hairy coat, a distinctive growl, a particular movement, an odor—any of these or any combination of these could trigger the appropriate set of responses to help us "avoid" an imminent attack, just as the rosy colors of ripening fruit and its sweet smell can alert us to initiate an "approach" response and move closer to investigate further a promise of food.

Can We Get Back to the Sex, Please?

Why does nonverbal communication deal only with survival, mating, and social signals? Those areas are the only ones where the correct response to signals will significantly increase fitness in an ecological niche and therefore increase the chance of survival. Clearly, if at one time there were animals that signaled their sex in their species alongside other animals that didn't, the first lot would meet and mate more often than the second, so eventually every member of the species would make those signals. However, our primitive signals suggest "mate *now*" and not "mate forever." And as many sales professionals look for long-term sales prospects, not short-term flings with the customer's purchasing power, our primal flirting signals though attention grabbing are shortsighted; and so getting ourselves as sales professionals stuck into the "sex" category will not likely increase our long-term sales "professional fitness." (This is not intended, however, to overlook the obvious power of sex in advertising, packaging, and some sales scenarios to initially alert and stimulate a buyer, the expertise around which would fill another book for marketing communications professionals.)

Equally, we can see that if prospective clients put us into the "enemy" category, they will be alert to us and wary of us. Then however we direct our verbal content toward them, even if we are saying words we think should be received as a benefit to them, our words will be framed within the context of "enemy," and they will avoid any positive relationship with our words, instead only able to view us and our content as potentially predatory. However, as we now know, we are by default likely to be shoved alongside our verbal message, product, or service, into the "indifferent" category; so not a "predator," but certainly not a "resource" either, and not an opportunity for procreation—therefore no immediate use to the survival of our prospective clients or their companies. This means we are simply not seen or heard again unless and until we send the right signals to get us into one of the three categories that get attention.

So our best option for creating and maintaining a long-term relationship with prospective clients that is positive for sales is to get ourselves firmly into the "friend" category: to show that we are there to supply to them, feed them, be of service in their quest for greater resources and ultimate survival. Exactly how we signal nonverbally in order to always fall into the friend category is the work of the next chapter.

Chapter 1 Quick Study

We believe and trust *what we see* more than anything else. If you produce nonverbal communication to members of your audience that you are a "friend," that is, you have resources for them, then you increase your prospects that they will open up to you and what you have to sell them. Equally, if you display body language that alerts the primitive brain that you are the "enemy"—in other words, a predator to their resources—they will close down to you and your offer. And if you don't appear as either of those—they probably just won't see you at all, unless they think you are sexy!

Great sales professionals act as our friends, not our enemies.

Just Do This Now

1. Look at the people immediately around you. Do you categorize them as "friend," "enemy," or "sex," or are you "indifferent" to them? What are their behaviors that currently cause you to categorize them as such?
2. Think about your best customers or clients and which category you would put them into.
3. Think about potential clients or customers whom you did not "hit it off with." What category did they touch on for you? And what might this mean going forward?

Theory to Practice

The graffiti artist Banksy says, "People either love me or hate me, or they don't really care." Regardless of whether *you* like him, dislike him, or have no idea who he is, he rather proves his point doesn't he?

Go into a public space and count the people who you feel have not noticed you—are indifferent to you. What must you do in order to quickly reduce that number—yet not cause people to be alarmed by you?

A Body of Knowledge

Jennifer La Trobe is the founding partner of Creative Connection (creativeconnection.ca), whose core offering is to recommend valuable problems. She and her partners, Tim Caswell (U.K.) and Chris Irwin (Canada), help their clients succeed by building awareness of the narrative and directing attention where it will be most effective. Here she talks about the roles we can most powerfully play in sales.

What on Earth Were You Thinking?

There is a philosophical supposition that our actions betray our beliefs. We can easily find examples in the actions of salespeople:

- The belittled female "car shopper" brings a male friend with her to the car lot in order to get serious attention. ("Do they think I can't buy a car alone?")
- The confused "computer shopper" feels patronized by being told what he should be looking for. ("Why can't someone ask me what I am using it for?")

- The frustrated "home renovator" is exasperated by being told that the choice among 60 odd countertop variations is "completely up to you." ("I come here for help and they give me none!")

Backing up from the observed action, can we assume that there are salespeople out there who firmly believe things like:

- Women don't buy cars alone.
- The average person has no clue what kind of computer they need.
- Who am I to tell you what kind of kitchen counter you want?

Guaranteed, these beliefs will have been well supported by evidence from past experiences. As the salesperson, you don't have to change your beliefs, but it is possible to put yourself in a different role in the story. If you have mastered the role of "expert," can you equally well portray one of these:

- Detective: can you solve the mystery of "The Perfect Countertop"?
- Facilitator: can you help this person work through their intimidation of technologies?
- Ally: can you partner with a driver to find the best car for her?

It starts between your ears, and it finishes in what you say, how you act, and how you move. The role you choose is largely up to you.

Annie Izmirliyan (williamvastis.com) is a wealth management coordinator with one of North America's top ranking advisors, working with individuals, families, and business owners to design a holistic wealth management experience. Here she talks about the attitude she takes toward body language to help her get clients to be most comfortable revealing sensitive personal and financial matters.

Financial Body

Always questioning the effects of body language in business relationships, I trained with Mark Bowden and found the answers I had been looking for. Those answers have not only made me aware of my instinctual reactions to events, situations, and people, but they also helped me consciously choose my behavior around others.

I work exclusively with high-net-worth clients. Regardless of the unique pressures that come from working with people of this status, there is a more universal challenge I face in planting with them the all-important seeds of trust, that no financial expertise, professional licenses, or designations can counter. when new clients first meet me they need to confide in me and reveal the most sensitive information about their families, their finances, and their dreams for the future. They must trust me.

Mark says that our brains subconsciously identify each other as being allies or friends quite instantly. So I need to be fully aware of not only the signals I am sending out to enhance our business's already trusted brand, but I also need to be fully aware of my own instinctual reactions to the client's communication, and then clear in controlling my responses in a way that helps our clients be most comfortable and open with me.

Winning Trust with a Wave of Your Hand

The Truth Behind Nonverbal Signals That Sell

> *Half the battle is selling music, not singing it.*
> *It's the image, not what you sing.*
>
> —Rod Stewart

In this chapter you'll learn:

- How to stay calm and assertive by selling from the TruthPlane
- The universal signals that command credibility immediately
- Neuroscience that connects you with your customers
- Exercises to test your new nonverbal skills
- Tips from a top performer

L istening to the advice of the average salesperson, motivational guru, or body language expert, each generally suggests that when selling under pressure, you are best to "grandstand" with a show of aggressive body language that suggests you are a powerful adversary who will not be shown the door—an "Alpha" with sales-professional-of-the-year invincibility.

Should you listen to this advice?

No—it's total hog. That's what makes it so average.

Instead, you are about to learn the key piece of nonverbal communication, understood in every culture around the world, that shows that you are nonconfrontational, open, available, and accepting of others' attitudes.

Some of you may well be thinking, "That's a weak strategy," and you'd be quite wrong. The prospective clients or customers at any presentation, meeting, store, or milling around at the trade show are not looking for someone who is going to outgun them. They are instinctively looking for someone who is going to help them, someone who is giving off the signals that he is a "friend," there to preserve and build everyone's resources, not deplete them. If you look as if you are out to diminish the status of others—be a predator to them—they will intuitively put you in the "enemy" category, and you will get a sharp response straight from their primitive fight-or-flight system: they'll retreat, attack, or just plain old play dead in front of you!

The Old Songs Are the Best

The following simple piece of body language, hundreds of thousands of years old, and still as applicable today as it ever was, has been totally overlooked by nonverbal communication "experts," sales presentation trainers, and motivational gurus around the globe. It has been handed down through an elite community of visual communicators across centuries and, until the publication of *Winning Body Language*, lacking any fully documented explanation of its powerful properties. It is only now with this book focused toward sales professionals like yourself that it might finally be able to be profited from commercially. So, to that end, here is the signal that instantly lets customers or clients know that your intention toward them is wholly benevolent and that you can be trusted implicitly:

Gesture on a horizontal plane extending from the navel.

Okay, so what you may be thinking now is, it can't be that simple! Yet, as you are about to experience and learn for yourself, it really is. And to prove it, let's do some practical work helping you more fully understand and experience the incredibly influential and persuasive powers of working within this "friend" position on the body, which we'll now call the *TruthPlane*. To get you there, let's first start in an entirely different horizontal plane of gesture, one that is widely used where the categories of "indifferent" and "enemy" get most played out.

Hands Down the Worst Exercise

Stand tall and upright but allow your hands to hang down by your sides (below the waistline) in what we call the GrotesquePlane of gesture (explanation of this shortly). Pay attention to your breathing rate. Note the pace and the quality of the breaths in and out that you are taking; for example, is your breathing slow-paced, fast-paced, or what you might describe as mid-paced? Do you feel as if you are taking in deep breaths, shallow breaths, or something you might describe as somewhere in between the two? Do you feel you are taking in a greater volume of air than you are breathing out, or vice versa, that you are breathing out a greater volume of air than you are breathing in?

As you stand, notice some details of your physical stance as a whole when your arms are hanging down on each side of your torso. How stable are your legs? How erect is your spine? How does your head feel right now on the top of your neck? How does your face feel? What are the muscles in your face doing, and what do you think is the nature of the expression shown by your mouth, your eyes, your forehead, and across your face as a whole? In addition to this, how do you *feel* right now? Describe that feeling to yourself; even name it if you can. Many people get a considerable feeling of "heaviness" in the physical, mental, and emotional sense. Consider whether that is what you are now feeling as well. Finally, take note of anything you experience beyond what has been outlined, and remember it all for comparison later.

Exercise Your TruthPlane

Again, make sure you are standing tall and upright. Now bring your hands up from your sides, where they were hanging, to your belly button, gently interlacing your fingers so that both your hands are held comfortably and lightly with your palms softly touching the navel area of your stomach. Can you immediately feel a difference in the way you are breathing? Is your breathing faster or slower than before? Has your breathing become deeper or shallower, or even perhaps more balanced? Do you feel that you are breathing out a greater volume of air than you are breathing in, or is there a sense of equilibrium to your breathing? Take any other note of how your breathing is now compared to how it was when your arms were hanging down by your sides.

Bringing your attention to your body as a whole: how are you standing right now? For example, how secure do you now feel in your feet and legs? How does this compare to how your stance was in the GrotesquePlane of gesture (i.e., when your arms were down by your sides)? What do you feel and think about the position of your spine and how your head now sits on your neck? Can you feel a difference, and if so, what makes up that important difference for you? Again, pay attention to your face. How do the muscles around your mouth, eyes, and forehead feel? What is the expression that you now feel that you have, and what feeling goes with that expression on your face? Can you describe the feeling it gives you to have your hands gently in the plane extending from your navel, and can you give that feeling a name? Also take note of anything else that you have experienced or thought since taking up this second position of the hands, especially in relation to your earlier experience of the GrotesquePlane.

Figure 2.1 Gesturing in the TruthPlane

Quickly drop your hands once again down by your sides into the GrotesquePlane. How fast do you revert to the original breathing pattern, stance, positioning, and feelings that go with this position? Now bring your hands up to your navel area and allow them to gesture anywhere in the horizontal plane that extends out 180 degrees from the center that is your navel (Figure 2.1). Be open with your gesture, giving clear access to the stomach (your elbows are bent, with some easy space under your arms, not flapping in the air, nor should they be digging into your sides). How quickly does the feeling that goes with the new physical position change?

Calm and Assertive

Many people describe the feeling they get from having their hands in the navel or the belly-button area (either hands interlaced or gesturing out) as being "centered," "controlled," "collected," "composed," or "calm" (generally a lot of things beginning with the letter *c*); but also, just as you will have experienced, they get a sensation of level-headedness, balance, and abundant energy.

Winning Body Language Theory

Why do we get a feeling of security and calm when we place our hands in this navel area (TruthPlane) and gesture from there? Why do we feel this equilibrium when gesturing from there as opposed to the feelings of lethargy and apathy many experience (setting ourselves up to get stuck in the *indifferent* category), or sometimes anxiety and aggression (preparing for battle, and so looking like an *enemy*), which comes when our hands are hanging in the Grotesque-Plane, whether to the sides, across our front, or clasped together around the back (or in our pockets)?

A primary reason is that just a couple of fingers' width below the belly button is the point where the sagittal, coronal, and transverse planes of the human body intersect. In Chinese and Japanese tradition (along with some Western sports practices), this is considered the physical center of gravity for the human body—a specific location at which the whole system's mass behaves as if it were concentrated. This center of mass is the point at which the whole of a body can be acted upon by gravity. Act upon a body's center of mass and in many cases you are very likely to act upon that whole body. As some engineers might agree, *the most productive input of energy to affect any mass is at its center*. So it is in the area of our navel, or belly button, that we have the most balanced center of gravity when we are standing still on firm ground. Hence the feeling of physical stability that is produced when you stand with your hands anywhere in this plane extending from that belly button region. Here you are aligning more of your mass to the center of that horizontal plane and so focusing your physical stability.

Selling It from the Stomach

The stomach is an important area of focus in sales communication skills for reasons that stretch beyond gesturing. Simply breathing from the stomach is a great way to feel at ease during a presentation. Before we can perform any action at all, we of course need oxygen as fuel. It is no surprise that the belly button or navel area plays an important, even essential role in breathing techniques practiced all over the world, from the Qigong's "embryonic breathing" and storage of vital Chi energy, to the foundation of any opera singer's powerful volume and range.

Another great example is in stage acting. "Breathing from the belly," which mainly involves controlling the muscles of the diaphragm, is an invaluable professional technique, the purpose of which is to draw air into the bottom portion of the lungs before the chest muscles expand and draw further air into the upper portion. This centuries old trick-of-the-trade dramatically increases lung capacity and therefore the amount of oxygen available from each breath, allowing a stage performer maximum vocal strength. Control of the diaphragm is also used to regulate the pressure and volume of air passed over the vocal cords, producing a more consistent and certain tone in the human voice.

And there is further convincing evidence for the powerful application of this technique within sales communication: this center point on the body, often called the "one point" or "dantien" (red wheel) in Eastern practices, is linked directly with the adrenal glands—the area hormonally responsible for the extreme stress response of "fight or flight."

Navel Intelligence

The adrenal glands are situated (as their name indicates, *ad* in Latin meaning "near," and *renes* meaning "kidney") on top of the kidneys and in front of the twelfth thoracic vertebra. The adrenal glands are chiefly responsible for regulating stress responses from your hormones. These hormones all play a part in the fight-or-flight response activated by the sympathetic nervous system. In simple terms, the adrenal glands link the thoughts of the brain to the physiological and physical action in the human body. They link to our primitive brain, but instead of thinking, just chemically react when stimulated.

So, whether you, as a sales professional, want to also join in with the ancient beliefs of the East or not, it is pretty clear from a couple of hundred years of modern Western endocrinology that the navel is indeed a control center for your biological mechanism for coping with stress. And certainly there are plenty of sales situations that get even the most experienced sales professional stressed out!

You Slay Me

On top of everything else, the stomach area is vulnerable to attack. Not only because, as you read earlier, it is the center of gravity—an attack in that area of the body can easily take a human to the ground, giving a predator further physical advantage and reducing any ability to escape—but because this part of the body holds some delicate organs that are unprotected by the rib cage (a protection the heart and lungs benefit from). We humans evolved from on-all-fours ground-dwelling mammals of the forest into upright walking Homo sapiens of the open African savannah. Our earliest ancestors benefited from the advantages this upright position had to offer of seeing long distances across the planes and catching the scent of food or predators over the distant winds; along with an added ability to exhaust prey by running them out over miles of open distance, and avoiding predators by being able to swiftly shift the body to one side.

But this progression upward also left the core of our movement and many of our most important digestive, endocrine, and excretory organs vulnerable. And so it is not surprising that when we are under stress, we respond by crunching our stomach muscles in to protect that vulnerable area—or simply move it away from any perceived threat. We certainly are not programmed with a pattern to expose this central area under threat of attack. Therein lies the most important implication of this gesture: when you consciously use gestures in the TruthPlane, both you and those around you have a natural response of *calm*, because a display from the TruthPlane means there is *no threat in the room*.

However you wish to look at it, the insight you need to take away from this unique "discovery" and documentation of the TruthPlane and how the environment—your own body included—affects your mind and the minds and moods of others (embodied cognition), is this:

> **When the hands gesture within the TruthPlane, an energized calm, confident, and balanced effect is felt by both the communicator *and the receiver.***

Not only does having your hands in this position affect *your* body language, but it also affects your whole nonverbal presence, and in turn the feelings your audience have about *you*, your attitude, and your intention.

And because of the interconnected nature of our physical system, your vocal tone is influenced by the GesturePlane you are in. Your actions become congruent with your intentions and feelings, and your vocal tone becomes calmer and gains a more trustworthy note, rhythm, and cadence. This is another reason why the technique is so effective—it changes one's voice quite profoundly and without the laborious vocal exercises that many other performance, presentation, and sales coaches recommend (only for you to then forget to perform when a feeling of pressure or crisis hits your sale). By using the simple technique of gesturing in the TruthPlane, you are utilizing your powerful preprogrammed reactions to simple body movements. Let's try it out.

An Exercise in Ordering Anxiety

It is time for you to experience the calm, confident, active effect of placing your hands within the TruthPlane while you are under conditions of stress. You are going to order a couple of pizzas from two different outlets.

Okay, you are thinking, what is so stressful about that? Well, here is the catch: you are going to walk into two retail stores, neither of which makes or sells pizza, or indeed any type of food or drink. A clothing store would be a good choice, or perhaps a bookstore. Because you know that entering a clothing store and asking the assistant for a pizza is potentially (if not definitely) embarrassing for you, this should cause your central nervous system to push your sympathetic nervous system into activating the stress-regulating arrangement of organs situated toward the back of your belly. Indeed, you should get a shot of adrenaline as you approach the store, and certainly a shot as you approach the counter or the fashion assistant with your food request.

For some of you, just imagining putting yourself in this situation will already bring on the adrenaline rush—that odd churning feeling in your stomach, dryness in your mouth, and the color draining from your face. So, for those of you who are unable to complete this exercise for whatever reason, you may try it in your imagination, because it may already be doing a great job of firing up your fight-or-flight response just as a thought experiment.

The GrotesquePlane

In the first store or shop, make sure you have your hands down by your sides in the GrotesquePlane. Try to monitor the level of stress and anxiety you feel, and take careful note of the type of response you get from the assistant. Understand that some of you may not even make it into the store because of the high levels of fear this exercise provokes!

The TruthPlane

Now for the second store: place your hands anywhere within the horizontal plane that extends at the height of your belly button. Allow about three ordinary breaths in and out with your hands in this area to balance out the oxygen levels in your bloodstream and restore equilibrium, particularly in light of your experience in the first store (or your experience outside of the store, for those of you who are, for whatever reason, acting out the physical instructions solely in your imagination).

Walk right into the store and keep your hands gesturing anywhere in the TruthPlane as you approach the service counter or assistant. When you ask for help with a pizza, be sure to gesture with your hands moving only within this horizontal plane. Keep your hands totally level on this horizontal plane that potentially spreads out a full 180 degrees from the center point of your belly button and goes out and beyond your personal space. Pay close attention to how you now cope with this stressful situation (or your imagined stressful situation), and pay close attention to the effect you feel you are having on the assistant this time around.

Debrief

Now that you've done this exercise, how did it go? How did you feel the second time around when your hands were stabilized in the belly area, as opposed to hanging by your sides in the GrotesquePlane when you approached the first shop? Did you feel more in control of your breathing the second time around (either for real or in your imagined encounter)? Did you feel more control over your feelings of stress the second time around? Did you notice any calmer reactions from the person with whom you spoke? (I'm sure you may have an understanding by now that presenting shop assistants with this moment of dissonance is extremely stressful for them too.) Did you find that this very simple piece of body language made an enormous difference to the situation, not only in providing you with stable feelings of balance, breathing, and bravery, but also in the type of reaction you got? Did others pay more calm attention to you?

Tone

What did you notice about the nonverbal element of communication in the tone of your voice when you were gesturing in the TruthPlane? Did you notice, as others often do, the calm and gently upward-inflecting tone, as opposed to the downward intonation of the GrotesquePlane? By now you will be starting to understand how making simple and clear decisions in the way you use your body language promotes clear decisions in the sound of your voice, along with clear decisions from others around you. You will also be getting the picture of how this simple idea of keeping your gestures within the TruthPlane affects how confident you feel and the confidence you display, not only in your body but in your voice. So let's look now at the most important factor in all of this: the effect that gesturing in the TruthPlane has on your potential clients and customers in sales situations of every kind.

Under the Influence

When you are under stress, you cannot stop your adrenal glands from doing their job because you cannot stop your brain stem from instructing them to do their job—the process is involuntary. Your reptilian brain is not under your conscious control, least of all in times of stress, when its purpose of saving your life really comes into its own. However, by physically keeping your gestures in the TruthPlane, you can effectively introduce a countermeasure to the reaction in the brain stem and in your adrenal glands. (Those of you who have tested this in the crazy pizza experiment should have real proof by now.)

And here's a really exciting part of this for anyone in sales interested in being persuasive and influential (and that should be *you*, by the way): you can now present this countermeasure to your natural reactions under stress and enable others to unconsciously mirror that countermeasure and reduce *their* stress along with you. Understand this: your prospective customers and clients are programmed at a deep level to *copy*. They are designed to copy the clear confidence (or to copy any feeling, for that matter) that you portray nonverbally, and to frame any verbal message with that same intention and emotional atmosphere through a process often referred to as "theory of mind."

Emotion, Mirrors, and Empathy

Being able to infer the intentions of other people is an extremely important ability for humans in their social interactions with others. It's a large part of what makes humans such a social species. Think of the advantage of being able to tell simply from the way someone else handles a rock whether he is just studying it or getting ready to throw it at you. Psychologists describe this ability as being part of a *theory of mind*. This is the idea that humans (and possibly a few other animals too) recognize that others have minds like their own and can make quite accurate hypotheses about the beliefs, desires, intentions, feelings, and mental states of others.

A primary way of establishing some theory of mind is of course in the way most people can easily read the emotions of others from subtle facial expressions and other, bigger physical behaviors. (This is of course what many call "body language.") This process of "reading" the emotions of others is initiated by cells in our brain, often referred to as *mirror neurons* (more about them later), that cause the stimulation of the muscular activities underlying these kinds of emotion-expressing behaviors.

Have you noticed how, if you imitate facial expressions or physical gestures and movement associated with emotional states (like fear, sadness, joy, etc.), you can actually start to feel at least a little bit of the emotion itself and sometimes get quite overwhelmed by it? Indeed, many professional actors use this "physical" method of acting in order to access a real—or as some might refer to it, "authentic"—emotional state of their own in order to project through the character in the drama they are playing. Of course, when you watch that performance on film, the actor's emotions ended long ago (likely soon after the director yelled, "Cut!"). But your theory of mind about the character's mental and emotional state, made up from your own mirroring of their physical state, creates an emotion in you that is transferred back onto the projection of the human (or monster, or animation, for that matter) on the screen. The character's emotions feel real—and they are. But that's because they are now *your* emotions. You have become "empathetic."

Empathy can be thought of as the ability to experience someone else's reality. "Mirroring" could most likely be described as the neural mechanism by which the actions, intentions, and emotions of other people can be automatically understood. Based on this theory, the recent discovery of mirror neurons (circa 1980) is considered by some as an important piece in the puzzle of how we connect with others and therefore how we are social. For communication to succeed, both the individual sending a message and the individual receiving it must recognize the significance of the sender's signal. Mirror neurons provide a mechanism for sharing the significance or meaning of the message, which can often not be encoded in the message itself.

Placing your hands in the TruthPlane is the single most effective way for the business communicator to fight back effortlessly against natural stress reactions and send out a clear signal to clients and customers that there is no problem and everyone can be confident. After all, why would you be displaying and drawing unconscious attention to this very vulnerable stomach area (both in terms of physical balance and unprotected vital organs) if you were under stress and, from your brain's point of view, "under attack"?

This is why not only do you feel more confident in this physical position, but others around you become more confident as well: they feel that you are confident, calm, stable and balanced, attentive, intelligent, and, most important, honest, authentic, and trustworthy. They become empathetic to your attitude, joining in and aligning with these feelings alongside you. You may even see them "mirror" your movements in the TruthPlane as a strong indicator that they are feeling just like you because they *like* the feelings you have and consequently they "like" *you*. You may also notice that in addition to mirroring your movements in the TruthPlane, they mirror your vocal intonation and the meaning associated with it. It has been observed that when a noise is heard, the motor neurons associated with the physical actions needed to create that sound are activated in the listener. For example, when we hear chewing noises, the neurons involved with moving the mouth are activated! So everything you do, including the way you speak, gets copied by the receivers' brain in an effort to identify a fitting action, intention, or emotion they have experienced themselves.

Taste Test

Here's a quick experiment: take a look at the two silhouettes in Figure 2.2 and ask yourself which person you trust more. Which of the two would you trust more if you were to hear the words from them, "It's a great product for you"?

Even with simple silhouettes, when the hands appear to be in the GrotesquePlane (the hands appear below the waistline), it's interesting that the viewer feels less assured and less trusting, compared with how we feel toward the silhouette with the hands at navel height (in the TruthPlane).

This is because of our reptilian brain, which is designed to look at simple body positioning and movement in order to make a quick decision as to whether the other person is a potential threat or a potential friend. Con-

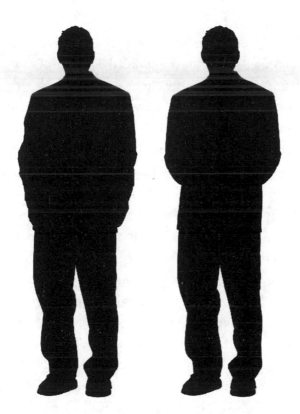

Figure 2.2   GrotesquePlane Versus TruthPlane

sidering the pictures, it may seem illogical for you to rate the two differently, because they both seem to lack a lot of clear information upon which to base a logical decision. But again, notice how remarkably easy it is for your unconscious process to quickly make a satisfactory decision as to which one you trust more, even though the figures are indistinct and monochrome.

Basic Body Mass Versus Cognitive Confusions

You can think of it this way too: in his book *Thinking Fast and Slow*, Daniel Kahneman talks about "System 1" and "System 2." System 1 is our *intuitive* brain, which drives a lot of our behavior and decision making, much more so than our System 2 *analytical* brain. System 2 is engaged when we are puzzled, confused, and forced to think deeply about something. As a salesperson, you do not want buyers to be puzzled, confused, and forced to think deeply about your intentions toward them. You want them to react to you in System 1—what Kahneman describes as "a place of cognitive ease": the nonstressful decision making our brain often prefers—this is the response the TruthPlane invites. By inhabiting the TruthPlane, it says to the buyer that you do not pose a threat; you are a friend and you are open. It creates an environment that invites engagement and dialogue. As a salesperson all you can ask when you begin the sales process is to start from a position that inspires trust.

You will be interested to know that contrary to many people's beliefs about what parts of the body are more important to us in how we interpret the emotions and intentions of others, facial features are initially not as important as the bulk of the body mass, particularly the position of the center of gravity and the hands. Scientific analysis has shown that a major part of emotional recognition as a prescreening device for social interaction comes from the body alone and excludes the face. The way people move their bodies tells us a lot about their feelings or intentions, and we use this information on a daily basis to communicate with each other.

News Flash

For an easy-to-see example of the power of using the TruthPlane to sell an idea or a concept or to give information about events and their meaning to you, just watch any TV reporter, presenter, or anchor delivering a piece of factual news: yes, that person's hands are in the TruthPlane. As professional communicators to a mass audience, many of these people unconsciously understand (or have been trained in the TruthPlane system) that if they place their hands at navel height, they will feel and sound more confident, and the viewers will feel confident with that anchor delivering the important "factual" information of the day. When people stand with their hands in the TruthPlane and deliver the story, we all start to feel that everything they are saying is factual. Yet we don't know why we're sure—we simply trust it. This is partly based on clear signals in body language and tone of voice as old as humankind, signals telling us that this human being (the reporter) is to be trusted, and therefore what she says is *selling* us the truth!

Try It Right Now

You should begin to use this most important body language gesture to win trust immediately. Try it right now with your friends and colleagues. Notice your confidence; notice the clear, calm quality in your voice; and notice the positive attention you get instantly. Notice others who do not use this plane of gesture when it would serve them well. Can you imagine how much better you would respond if they were selling to you from the TruthPlane? Decide right now how you are going to use this powerful secret of winning body language to your immediate advantage when you make your sales calls today, and then read on for much, much more.

Chapter 2 Quick Study

Benefits of gesturing in the TruthPlane: the primal stress response experienced by both you and the receivers of your sales message when you communicate under pressure, or in a situation of "indifference" to your message, can be counteracted by *placing your hands anywhere on the horizontal plane that extends out 180 degrees from a center of the navel—or, as we call it, the TruthPlane.* Open gestures in this plane are the most effective way to engender trust with other humans in microseconds.

Just Do This Now

When you communicate, place your hands as much as possible in the TruthPlane—the horizontal plane that extends out from the navel area; in anatomical terms, at the "Transverse Plane" or "Axial Plane" that divides the body into cranial and caudal—head and tail—portions.

Use the TruthPlane to cause your body and mind to be calm during sales communications.

Lead your prospects, clients, or customers to become confident in you and in themselves and their decisions by placing your hands and gestures open in the TruthPlane when you communicate with them, unconsciously framing their access to your vulnerable belly area.

Theory to Practice

Grab a video camera; your smartphone will do fine. Pick a topic for a short story—your last round of golf, a current event, what happened during the drive home today, anything simple. Set the camera up to record you speaking. Now, while you are recording yourself, tell the story first with your hands in the GrotesquePlane, at your sides—do not lift them above your waist. Then tell the same story from the TruthPlane.

Now looking back at the two videos, what was the difference?

In the GrotesquePlane, you may notice that you were possibly struggling to find the words and add any interest or color to the story. Compared with your story in the TruthPlane, it was most probably boring and dull, and you may even have almost fallen asleep during it. In the Truth-Plane, everything was easier; the ideas in the story came to mind more quickly and were easier to share. The story was most probably more interesting too, and you were more engaged as a viewer watching it back.

If you do this experiment again but choose two different stories, you will find that any viewer will remember a lot more of the details of the story told in the TruthPlane than the story told in the GrotesquePlane.

A Body of Knowledge

Shaun Prendergast (represented by Wintersons—nikiwinterson.com) is one of the United Kingdom's most renowned performers and a founding member of Kenneth Branagh's Renaissance Theatre Company. He holds a distinguished career in film, television, and theater internationally, both as an actor and a writer. He trains performers at the Royal Court Theatre and Sir Paul McCartney's Liverpool Institute of Performing Arts, and he works with performers such as Sting. Here Shaun talks about how a knowledge of your own physicality can help you understand if you might be unwittingly putting other people "on ice" toward you.

Cold Comfort

Body language is an essential part of acting because all of us have a physical life, a set of movements, stances, and physical attitudes that communicate our thoughts and attitudes to others. Obviously, if you're playing a character, it's essential to work out what they would be communicating, consciously or unconsciously, and to develop a physical life that belongs to the character.

To illustrate this: I was once being directed by Dame Judi Dench alongside Kenneth Branagh. Judi said that whenever the character I was playing entered onto the stage, she wanted it to be like there was "a cold draft in the room." I found this difficult—I'm a gregarious, party guy. That night Mark Bowden came to dinner and we talked about my character (Don John from *Much Ado About Nothing*), how he felt, his bitterness, and the ways I could show this through his behavior. The next day, in rehearsal, I had developed a way of moving that was still, self-composed, and very deliberate.

Nothing wasted, and most importantly for the feeling of icy coldness, absolutely nothing given away. Not a word was said, but it was obvious to every member of the audience how Don John got no pleasure from life.

Working with Mark, I had understood how to analyze my own body language and to notice other people's and what it said about them too. Just like if you're buying something, you look for openness, honesty, and friendliness—not closed, coldhearted, and "disdained of all."

Types and Territory

Sales People and the World of Sales

*There are two kinds of people in the world: those who divide
the world into two kinds of people, and those who don't.*
                                        —Robert Benchley

In this chapter you'll learn:

- How to manage the risks of the "salesperson" stereotype
- Ways to physically categorize your customers to help them buy
- How territory affects "fight and flight" with your clients
- The "upper-hand shake" to win trust on first contact
- Three ways to open your heart to buyers

L ife is so much easier for us when we can consciously put people into boxes: categorize them by knocking the less discernible or more problematic edges off, and then putting them into a pigeonhole—typecasting them for the role we expect them to play throughout the sales process and maybe throughout our lives in general. Indeed, it takes so much less neural resource to do this that it is precisely what our brains do for us by default.

You have now heard about how the primitive brain makes its first snap judgments and determines if we are "friend," "enemy," "potential sexual partner," or is otherwise "indifferent" to us. You are no doubt learning to be more conscious of your own nonverbal behavior and have perhaps tried projecting yourself into one of these categories by choice rather than as the subject of unconscious reactions of others. You can now choose to use more effective body language in order to have the best opportunity of being placed in the "friend" category by using the TruthPlane when you meet, help, or present to a client or customer.

And so in this chapter we will begin to think about how we judge others, and how we may be judged by others on a more subtle level, with respect to ideas we all carry with us about "personality types." We'll look at how this knowledge can translate into powerful body language techniques to manage ourselves and others throughout the sales process.

In a Class of Your Own

When we talk about *personality type*, we are often referring to some idea of a psychological classification based on a theory that we have about other people's state of mind, an explanation of why they take the actions they do, why they behave in a particular way. Some of these classifications may be based on science, some on personal experience, some on intuition, and some on pure guesswork (and some perhaps from the astrology column of the *National Enquirer*).

Whatever your method, these judgments are not necessarily correct nor are they necessarily incorrect. Many of the instinctual "gut reactions" we have of others are spot-on correct; some newspaper horoscopes sum up the reasoning behind others' behavior in spookily accurate ways. Equally, some of these judgments are totally out of whack, even those made on the most scientific basis. In all judgments there are risks. The job of this chapter is to help you manage the risks inherent in the subtler judgments people make about you based on your nonverbal behavior, along with the risks inherent in the judgments you make about your prospective and current buyers based on how you see them too.

System Thinking

There are many systems out there that seek to quantify and/or qualify the differences between people that often prove helpful to employers and managers who feel they can gain some advantage by being alerted to some of the risks and benefits that come with various "types" of people. You may very well have been assessed by one of these systems at one or more times in your career.

Some of these assessments see the differences in human personality as "either/or": e.g., someone may be seen as either an introvert or an extrovert; alternatively, some others see traits as part of a continuum—where you can be somewhere on a sliding scale between say an extrovert and introvert. As with all models, even if incorrect, they can be useful because they are at least a starting point to thinking more deeply about others and their actions, and more importantly, about *yourself*. The downside would be that such models can be used to justify quick decisions about others based on a limited, distorted, or deleted map of their humanity. Some of those less thoughtful decisions can turn out wrong (just as some of the more thoughtful ones turn out wrong too).

So how can we simplify our understanding of people to a useful degree in order to start thinking about them quickly and clearly and then work toward nonverbally influencing their behavior to buy from us?

Jung? He Was When He Started!

One of the most influential ideas concerning personality originated in the work of famous psychologist Carl Jung. His theories on different fundamental psychological attitudes led him to categorize people into primary types of *psychological function*, expressed in either an "introverted" or "extroverted" form.

According to Jung, extraversion (also commonly spelled "extroversion") means "outward turning"; and perhaps unsurprisingly, "introversion" means "inward turning." These specific definitions vary somewhat from the popular usages of the words (for example, words like "gregarious" for extrovert and "introspective or quiet" for introvert are commonly used). A human being's preference for extroversion or introversion is often called an "attitude." Cognitive function (i.e., thinking) can operate in the external world of behavior, action, people, and things (extroverted attitude) or the internal world of ideas and reflection (introverted attitude).

Jung's model says that people who prefer extroversion *draw energy* from action: they tend to act, then reflect, then act further. If they are inactive, their motivation tends to decline. To rebuild their energy, extroverts need breaks from time spent in reflection. Conversely, those who prefer introversion *expend energy* through action: they prefer to reflect, then act, then reflect again. To rebuild their energy, introverts need quiet time alone, away from activity. In short: the extrovert's energy is directed outward toward people and objects, and the introvert's is directed inward toward concepts and ideas.

You can no doubt see how in any sale there is a benefit to extroverted behavior and a benefit to introverted behavior from both the sales professional and the buyer. It is fair to say that the salesperson stereotype is that of the extrovert, and that indeed many great sales professionals and role models in sales lean that way. But you can recognize that sometimes it is imperative to lean toward introverted behavior, for example when the buyer needs to be led in reflecting upon concepts and ideas. Just as it is essential to be able to lead introverts through a more extroverted set of behaviors—moving them into external action around the buying process, as with physically testing the product or service by consciously moving into that attitude yourself. Well, here's how you can do just that.

Shut the Front Door

Here is a technique that has been kept secret for quite a while now. This technique did not even make it into *Winning Body Language*! Not because it is not a powerful technique—far from it. Rather, because the right professional audience of salespeople and specific context were needed for its introduction. So think about the following exercise carefully, and then, even better, do it now:

Standing up, imagine that you have a line going from your ear to shoulder, down your hips, down to the anklebone. This line divides your body laterally. Using your imagination, transform that line into a two-dimensional plane that cuts the body into two. The front of your body—face, chest, stomach, kneecaps, and toes—is in front of that plane. The back of your head, the back of your neck, your back, behind the backs of your legs and heels, are all behind that bisecting plane.

Now, concentrate on your center of gravity, the point a couple of inches down and a couple of inches in from your navel. Imagine that that point is dead center on the plane cutting your body in half laterally. You can think of it this way too: imagine a door frame, and as you step into that frame, get yourself in the exact center, positioning your center of gravity

Figure 3.1 The DoorPlane

so it is in a place where the door frame—if transformed into a bisecting plane—would cut through your center. Now you are at the center of what we will now call the "DoorPlane™" (Figure 3.1).

How does it feel? Do you feel calm and assertive? Do you feel a sense of strength? This is the kind of general feeling that many, many people get when they are at the center of the DoorPlane.

Now feel your center as you move it in front of the DoorPlane—just a couple of inches, maybe (keep your feet still for now). Can you now feel a surge of energy moving you forward? Do you feel like moving (although you are sitting or standing still)? Move your center even farther forward of the DoorPlane and feel the surge of more aggressive energy come into you. Is this a feeling you have when you are in "sales mode"? Now bring yourself back to the center of the door plane and feel the calm and assertive feeling come back to you. Feel how it is more of a neutral place to be. A better place to listen from perhaps, and certainly not instilling in you the feeling of "going in for the kill," as when you are far in front of the DoorPlane.

Now let's experience being behind the DoorPlane. Center yourself in the DoorPlane and get the feeling for that: calm and assertive, available and adaptable, resilient yet open to change. Now pull your center to just an inch or two behind the DoorPlane and notice the feeling of "retreat" or "avoid" that it might give you. Can you already sense what some would see and describe as an "introverted" nature, as opposed to the more outwardly energized or extroverted feeling of being in front of the DoorPlane? Often, people find the resulting physicality of being behind the DoorPlane more thoughtful or inward looking—reflective.

Now pull your center even farther back from the DoorPlane and see how this affects your feelings. Can you feel that you are now closing down to the outside and becoming more cautious and self-conscious? When have you felt like this in a sales situation? How useful to the sale might this feeling have been? A guess is that this more extreme introversion is often not so useful for the sales situation. So now pull yourself back to the center of the DoorPlane and notice how your feelings quickly change back to being calm and assertive again. Push your center forward and notice how you quickly get energized and aggressive in comparison.

Notice how you are in charge of these states and feelings of being passive or aggressive when you physically take charge of your body language. Now remember from Chapter 2 how those around you are designed to mirror you. What do you think you could achieve if you use this technique to affect your own state when selling, and in turn affect the buyers around you?

Big and Small

Mike Bosworth, the author of *Solution Selling,* used to conduct a short thought experiment early in his sales training seminars to help train salespeople in how to be more relevant and effective when selling to executives. He would draw two stick figures facing each other on a flip chart—one large, the other small. He would then invite the audience to identify the salesperson in the picture. Before you read on, conduct the experiment for yourself; take a look at the diagram in Figure 3.2 of the two stick figures facing each other. For you, which of the two figures is the salesperson and which is the customer? Which is you and which is the customer?

Figure 3.2   Who Is Selling to Whom?

The way you initially see this might say something about how you instinctively, or perhaps culturally, feel about yourself within a buyer/seller relationship. But the real purpose of the experiment is to illustrate that the minute you come into a situation as a salesperson, you ignite a reflexive response in the buyers based on *their* stereotypes or quick and simple judgments about "salespeople."

In the case of some, it might be that whenever they come into contact with a salesperson, they lose respect for and are conditioned to look down upon them—see them as "small." The result is that everything the salesperson says will likely be seen as not terribly credible, even viewed with suspicion. Alternatively, for others the salesperson may trigger a response of feeling small, fearing that this person might bully them into spending on something they do not want or need.

For the salesperson, everything about this binary big/small classification situation is bad news. If the buyer decides to align himself with the large figure, then the seller will need to work to assert herself as an equal. If the buyer selects the small figure, the salesperson needs to be careful not to intimidate the buyer and scare him away. And it gets more complex if you are meeting with a group that has a mix of feelings!

From the perspective of body language and nonverbal communication, the implied question is: "How do we work within these emotional realities of the buyer, and not trigger the wrong reaction?"

The Doors of Perception

Go back to the feelings you got practicing the techniques from the Door-Plane exercise and notice how "in front of the door" feels "big." Think how it would feel to sell, pitch, or present to a customer from this position. Do you think your clients or customers would themselves be big or small when you presented yourself to them with this physicality and feeling? Now step a good two feet in front of the door and feel the surge of energy. How big and powerful do you feel now? Maybe you are feeling quite aggressive so far in front of the door, with the sensation that those around you are smaller and really need to "get out of your way."

Now see how easily you can dial that feeling back by centering yourself once again in the DoorPlane. In fact, dial it right back by stepping a foot behind the door. How different does this now feel?

Do you agree that somewhere in the center of the DoorPlane lies the starting point for being physically and mentally *available* for consulting with your client toward a sale?

All the World's a Stage

During a sale, you may need different orientations of "size" or status in relation to your client. At some stages in a sale you may need to encourage buyers to engage with you in an open, equal way. At other stages you may need to take command of the situation and be "big" in order to be most helpful to them. And there are equally some moments during the process of a sale that would benefit from taking a "small" approach in order to influence them forward.

Using your ability to orient yourself within the DoorPlane, you can quickly dial your size up or down in relation to your customer or client, and even in relation to the broader definition of space you are inhabiting—because you also need to manage how you make that impression on and within the bigger environment as a whole, including the space, objects, and other people who are external to the client or customer. You need to control how you affect the whole territory around you, sometimes under the most difficult of circumstances.

Territorial Triggers and Trust

When we are under stress, we can easily stake a claim on whatever resources we believe are ours (and maybe some we think should be ours) for the taking—those of immediate use. However, for any sales professional, it is essential to present a physicality to others that does not fire off a reaction in their primitive brains warning them that their territory is being invaded. Messages that can suggest you are "taking over" include leaning on, touching, or standing in close proximity to another person's perceived property (which includes just about everything—fixtures, stationery, computer equipment, furniture, and even people). Leaning against an object that is likely deemed to be in their territory, while seemingly innocent enough, can be perceived as dominating and intimidating. Observing someone leaning against a wall or hanging in a doorway or a passage can make us feel that that person is displaying an attitude of ownership over that exit, entry point, or pathway. The person comes across as too big for the space—taking up too much territory—which could definitely cause others to feel small in return.

Taking a look at Abraham Maslow's Hierarchy of Needs, he posits that the fundamentals of territorial behavior center around our basic survival needs, all of which are to be found in the bottom two tiers of the hierarchy: the first of these tiers covers physiological needs, i.e., air, water, food, sleep, sex, and the basic bodily functions; the second tier up covers safety needs, like security and stability in areas such as health, employment, resources (including property), and allies. Maslow felt that unfulfilled needs in a lower tier would inhibit the person from gaining satisfaction on the next level. His illustration: "Someone dying of thirst quickly forgets their thirst when they have no oxygen."

We can apply this model and way of thinking to sales: someone whose territory is being invaded, and so feels that his status is being chipped away at, is unable to listen effectively to and appreciate your sales presentation.

Within the neuroscience and chemistry of engagement, the human brain is constantly scanning for clues as to whether a situation holds risk or reward. Our brains are therefore looking for how we might rank in relative importance to others (i.e., our status) by judging the perceived resource others have in relation to what we have. The brain asks: "Does this environment give me a high rank (plenty of resources) or a low rank (a deficiency of resources)?"

If the brain perceives it has a "high rank" and so high status, it triggers a reward response by delivering elevated levels of the "feel good" neurotransmitter *dopamine* to the brain, which in turn triggers an "approach" response in the body (in some cases the whole body literally moves forward). Incidentally, in this case the actual physical environment gets placed firmly in the mind into the "friend" category.

Conversely, a decrease in perceived resources, and thus a lowering of rank or status—as assigned by the environment—triggers a threat response, and the actual environment gets put into the "enemy" category. In this case, levels of dopamine are depressed, which in turn triggers an "avoid" response where individuals will physically and mentally retreat from the environment. Again, this reaction can be so bold that they literally walk out of the room.

Establishing Your Territory in a Room

Therefore, how you treat the space, orient yourself and others within a room or around a table, is vitally important as to how comfortable others feel about their own status or rank within the territory. As well as staying clear of claiming a stake to exits and other important points in the room, watch out for objects such as furniture and fixtures that create barriers between you and your clients or customers.

Physical barriers blocking you from your clients will also block your ability to use the most effective body language for getting into and staying in the "friend" category: others cannot see your *open* hand gestures (an open hand being the primitive signal of "no tools—no weapons," explained later in this chapter) unless your hands are over the top of the furniture, and so often at chest height. At this height (in what we call the PassionPlane— read on for more detail), the sales professional is more likely to go over the top emotionally and become overly passionate or too direct.

You should consider moving away from the furniture into more open space, in order to show your openness (both literally and metaphorically). Also, if you are seated while selling, pull your chair back from the desk or table and make sure it is high enough so you are communicating from your TruthPlane over the top of the table. This will relax the people around you: they now have access to your vulnerable stomach area, and you look confident.

For a good example of communicating effectively while sitting behind a desk, think again of the behavior of a news anchor. The news anchor's desk is always set at a height at which the hard copy of the news sits on top of the desk, and consequently cuts directly in at the anchor's TruthPlane. Furthermore, the anchor's hands rest on the desk at belly height. There is no mistake or coincidence in this placement: the image we get is that the news reader is trustworthy and that the news is fact and not simply subjective editorial opinions. News entertainment uses this image in order to place the anchor firmly in the "friend" category for a viewer's primitive brain.

The PassionPlane

Place your hands in the TruthPlane and monitor your approximate breathing rate and the extent to which you are filling your lungs with air. You will probably notice that when your hands are in the Truth-Plane, you are breathing steadily and fairly deeply—right down into your diaphragm. Now shift your hands up to your chest height and notice the difference. What has happened to your breathing rate? Into which part of your lungs are you predominantly bringing oxygen? You will have noticed that when you set your hands in the chest area—specifically the horizontal plane of gesture that comes out from just a couple of inches above the sternum (the center and bottom of the rib cage, at exactly the level at which you can best feel your heartbeat)—your breathing rate quickly increases and you breathe more into your chest than in your belly. Some of you may have already noticed an increase in your heart or pulse rate that automatically goes along with this.

It seems that gesturing with your hands at chest level automatically increases your breathing rate and heart rate and produces a slightly shallower style of breathing. Also, try talking: do you notice the increased upward inflection of the voice? This implies nonverbally that there is still more to come: it creates tension and suspense, causing any listener to be hooked into the sound in order to hear it completed with a downward ("it's over") tonality.

By using this upward intonation, you are instigating the members of your audience to demand completion of the musical cadence, and they will be hooked until they are satisfied. Do you also notice that your body feels more suspended? There may be a feeling of "something is about to happen" when you have your hands up, gesturing in the chest area. The mirroring or copying that you by now know to expect from your listeners causes their breathing to also be suspended. They are now looking for a deep outbreath and will remain hooked by you until you let them off the hook by giving a strong outbreath accompanied by an instruction for action. And with all the energy that your performing in this state has built up in them, there is a surplus of energy they need to expend with action (or risk a build-up of toxins).

Your call for action is all the excuse the body needs to redress their energetic balance by getting up and going for it. The excitement of the energy you are creating, both in your body and in the tone of your voice, is bestowed upon the verbal content of your speech.

When your hands come up to your chest and you gesture and speak (Figure 3.3.), there is an energetic buzz, particularly in contrast to the loss of energy and potential depression in the Grotesque-Plane and the level-headed stability of the TruthPlane. Gesturing from the chest area literally raises your oxygen level, and thus your energy level, gets your blood pumping from your heart, and compels those around you to do and feel the same. This is why we will call this area the *PassionPlane*.

Figure 3.3   Selling in the PassionPlane

Colorful Salespeople Versus Dull Customers

Levels of trust can go up as well as down depending on how passive or aggressive you are, or are perceived to be by the others in the room, and depending on the situation. This is an especially complicated system to navigate and manage for the sales professional. Salespeople are often thought of, stereotypically, as aggressive, "extroverted" (as discussed above), often gregarious. If we look at one aspect of this salesperson stereotype, they are *expressive* communicators.

Drs. Robert and Joyce Hogan, widely credited with demonstrating how personality factors influence organizational effectiveness, came up with an assessment system for personality and behavior that is relevant to this discussion. One dimension of Hogan's Leadership Challenge Survey is "color." Color is loosely translated as a person's impact on an audience or a room. Salespeople typically have personalities with high scores on the color scale.

The challenge this may impose on an organization is that a salesperson with a really high color score is one who dominates the room at the expense of all others. Wherever you score on this color scale, as a salesperson you probably have been doing a reasonable job with expressive communication. However, you will find that many buyers score near zero on the color scale. These people are low reactors, passive participants in a conversation, especially if they are facing a "fast-talking salesperson." The job for the salesperson of gaining the trust of the buyers in these situations is to draw these low reacting, potentially "introverted" personalities into an engaged and trust-filled dialogue without triggering all the "avoid" responses potentially associated with the salesperson stereotype effect.

The opposite pressure exists when facing buyers who would score high in color. They will naturally lean toward dominating the conversation and may insist on leading that conversation. The challenge for the salesperson is to influence the flow of the conversation with high-color buyers without overtly challenging their authority and taking their territory. The key is to get and maintain an equal status, and again win their trust.

You can now watch out for whether your customers or clients are "in front of the door" or "behind the door" or in their neutral position. If there is a need to be more "colorful" than your clients, then push yourself farther in front of the DoorPlane. If you need to dial back the color in relation to the buyers, then bring yourself to neutral or just a touch behind the DoorPlane. If you wish to show an equal rank to them in how colorfully you communicate, then consciously mirror the levels to which you feel their center is either in front of or behind the DoorPlane.

Watch also for the degree that your customers or clients are in the PassionPlane. High on the color score often goes hand in hand with the PassionPlane, and low on the color score may find them gesturing in the GrotesquePlane. Again, you can mediate and regulate the situation by elevating or lowering your gestures accordingly, along with noting how your proximity to them within the territory may be pushing your relative color higher or lower.

Let's go into more ways to think about relationships and space.

Distance Learning

The details of the ways we treat territory, and a group (or groups) within it, are mapped out in the work of anthropologist Edward Hall, who has a great rule that describes his theory on the effects of people being close to or far away from each other, or "proxemics," as it became known: "Like gravity, the influence of two bodies on each other is inversely proportional not only to the square of their distance but possibly even the cube of the distance between them." So, the closer you come to people, the greater your influence over them, and, of course, the greater their influence over you.

Body spacing and posture, according to Hall, are unconscious reactions to often subtle changes in nonverbal communication. The social distance between people, he believed, could be reliably correlated with physical distance, i.e., people of equal status will gravitate toward each other, and so be physically closer than those of unequal status; just as the closer you are to someone emotionally, the closer you become physically.

Note the delineations made by Hall in his *American Anthropologist* article, "A System for the Notation of Proxemic Behavior":

- Intimate distance, used for embracing, touching, or whispering: close phase, less than 6 inches (15 cm); far phase, 6 to 18 inches (15 to 45 cm)
- Personal distance, used for interactions among good friends: close phase, 1.5 to 2.5 feet (45 to 75 cm); far phase, 2.5 to 4 feet (75 to 120 cm)
- Social distance, used for interactions among acquaintances: close phase, 4 to 7 feet (1.2 to 2.1 m); far phase, 7 to 12 feet (2.1 to 3.6 m)
- Public distance, used for public speaking: close phase, 12 to 25 feet (3.6 to 7.5 m); far phase, 25 feet (7.5 m) or more

If we apply these guidelines to selling, the farther you are from your client, the less social, personal, or intimate effect you are likely able to have upon her. Some experts have called this phenomenon "exponential attraction." Therefore, we might say that in order to make a greater impact on the members of your audience, you must have spatial intimacy with them, and so one would guess that you should move toward them (and there are many communication coaches who say exactly that).

However, we must bear in mind how easy it is to cross important boundaries of spatial acceptability; as we have been looking at with respect to status infringement through accidentally laying claim to another person's territory by "getting in his space." It is simply not enough to say, as some do, that "trust increases when we move closer to people" or that you should "move into personal space to make key points with greater impact." You run the risk of intimidating your customers and lowering their status with this move, either by moving too close into their territory or, if you have a natural height advantage, through towering over them, or looming over them seated (as though you have the "higher ground," so to speak).

One way to instantly overcome the potential for lowering of status due to proximity or simply height is to (in the Western business culture) *shake hands*. But in the right way! Remember earlier in this chapter you were introduced to the idea of making customers and clients comfortable by using open hand gestures (the primitive signal of "no tools—no weapons"). Well, read on to understand how the secret of a great handshake is to "give them the upper hand."

Disarming or Alarming

Although the handshake is egalitarian, this simple cultural norm is often used today to show dominance. Some people, for example, in certain circumstances, will give you (consciously or unconsciously) a "crushing" handshake in order to display their greater physical strength relative to yours. Other people will unconsciously employ a flaccid grip to give you the idea that you have more strength than they do—in other words, to demonstrate their submission. However, if during a handshake, either (or both) party does not get to feel the palm of the other's hand—that is, if full contact is not made in the area of flesh between the thumb and the index finger of both parties, and so the palms also do not get a good full contact—this instantly causes a reaction of movement away from you, the now potential threat. In short, it is alarming not to feel the palm of the other person's hand in a handshake.

Try it out with a friend or a good work colleague; it is most interesting with someone you know and trust fairly well, because when you shake hands with him and do *not* make contact with the palm of your hand, you will notice a very quick change in your friend's face, maybe even a universal facial display of disgust, fear, or even surprise. Even though the two of you know and trust each other to a higher degree than most, the unconscious mind, which is protecting us second by second, does not take this fact into account. The unconscious mind perceives only that there is information it does not have, and therefore it is unhappy—the result is "retreat, be cautious, or attack."

Clearly, to build trust, an effective handshake should always make good full contact palm-to-palm. And not only can you build trust with something as simple as the right handshake, but you can also raise the status of another person without lowering your own. But first, what not to do.

With good palm contact, it is possible to shake hands in such a way that you become dominant, thus lowering the other person's status and making him shut out your message: simply turn his hand slightly over during the handshake so your palm is on top of his. This gives you more control of the other's arm (i.e., not that you would, but this puts you in the position that you could easily push your whole weight down on his arm and control it, making it difficult for him to bring his weight and center of gravity upward to push up against gravity and your arm's strength).

When you have the "upper hand" in a handshake, you put the other party at a physical disadvantage. You have "one-upped" him, lowered his status, and now he may be fleeing from you or fighting you. Try this with a friend or colleague and see what happens, both in his facial expression and full body language. Do you notice the aggression (locked eye contact, squaring off of the shoulders, and so on)? Or do you see him become passive (dropping eye contact and lowering the head, along with some folding in at the stomach and across the shoulders, and maybe even a step back)?

Also notice what happens if you push your upper hand along with your colleague's closer toward and nearly touching his stomach area—right into his TruthPlane, in fact, one of the most vulnerable areas of the body. Do you notice how your friend instantly becomes more passive? Even if your friend might have been aggressive at first, once your hand moves into this very vulnerable area of the body, his unconscious mind knows he has been compromised, and it will wait for further instructions from the higher-status individual (you, in this case). You could even now put your left hand on his right elbow, taking control of his forearm. This handshake is almost as controlling as any "greeting" can get, and using it is the secret to losing friends and alienating people! Get someone to give you this handshake so that you can feel how bad it is to receive it, and by doing this, you'll stand a great chance of never, ever, accidentally or on purpose, doing it to anyone else. It should be reserved only if you have such a great business that you wish to lose deals from the onset, or when as a leader you have come to the realization that you are a master of the universe and all should quake in your presence!

Of course, knowing all this, you can use the opposite version of this technique to give the other person status. Doing so instantly raises his engagement with you because of the sheer unconscious pleasure it gives. What if everytime you met someone, you could now make him feel like a million dollars? Here's all you have to do to make people feel that way: when you shake hands, simply offer your hand first with your palm facing up, so the other person's hand lands on top of yours. Then *gently* move both your and his clasped hands closer toward and into your vulnerable stomach area (right at a level with your belly button—your TruthPlane); you can do this by stepping gently forward into the handshake. Try this out and you will be truly astonished at how the corners of your friend's mouth instantly turn up into a smile and he steps in toward you, making great eye contact. He feels good with you and so relaxes. And when someone feels good with you, then everything around you, including the message you are giving, is good. This is a particularly attractive habit for physically imposing and "high color" salespeople. When you meet others on the extrovert side of the equation, or who are smaller in stature, give them status, roll your palm in the handshake up slightly and draw them ever so slightly into your TruthPlane. You will help them relax and open the doors to trust.

If you continue to physically dominate others, you stand a good chance of causing the fight-or-flight response in them. We are all looking for a strong person who will be on our side—not one who will be against us.

Reading Them Like a Book

As you've been reading this chapter, you might have noted that even when you categorize humans into a binary set of "types"—introverted/extroverted, big/small, colorful/dull, passionate/passive, etc.—human interaction during your sales process is still a complex system to manage, and at the end of the day is largely based on assumptions we make.

It is a big risk when we go into the business of attempting to "read" the body language of others to get intelligence (and not what we focus on in this book, opting instead to arm ourselves with the best body language tools to make ourselves more effective communicators)—since "reading" is based on your perspective and not theirs. Given this, what is the most foolproof way to assess someone else's body language to get a useful sense of his or her internal state?

The best question to ask yourself in order to glean some understanding of the body language of someone else is to question whether that person seems "open" or "closed" to you. What kind of detail is the unconscious mind looking for? It checks to see what is happening in the face. For example, are the eyebrows up and open? If so, this leaves the eyes on display and therefore vulnerable; if the eyes are vulnerable, it stands to reason that the person may be open to you, that is, she does not see you as a threat. Is there a gentle smile on the lips? Remember that the smile is a signal for "is good now." Again it stands to reason that if a person has a gentle smile (not a massive toothy and therefore potentially aggressive grin), she is open to you—she feels that situation is good now.

Think also about the body at large. Is it oriented toward you or away from you? Are the gestures they make relatively open at the belly? Again, if the torso is exposed toward you, then it stands to reason they are open to engaging with you, i.e., they see you as a benefit and not as a threat. Now of course none of these gestures mean with 100 percent certainty that a person is open to you, just as the opposite scenario—a closed face, closed body—does not absolutely mean that the other person is therefore closed to you. Indeed, it has been seen in scientific testing that the conscious reading of body language by anyone other than the most expert of experts, and even then only when this expertise is included in a wider intelligence system, is there any possibility of having a better than 50-50 chance of reading body language correctly.

However, your unconscious mind is brilliant at sending you a *feeling* that can help you judge someone else's feeling. Trust your gut reaction, instincts, and your feelings about a situation, and then test that in the sales situation by questioning, and using your own body language to adapt and influence the situation toward the sale. When you have mastered that with one other person, you could be ready to try it out with a whole new tribe of people.

Chapter 3 Quick Study

Personalities are complex, to say the least. However, it can be useful to make quick judgments about whether people are open or closed to you, aggressive toward you, or passive in the sale. Having these judgments can help you decide in the moment how you need to act in order to lead them in the best direction for the sale. But beware . . . people are also territorial animals. You must be respectful of that territory or you will cause them to retreat or advance aggressively with respect to you and your ideas.

Just Do This Now

1. Use the DoorPlane to judge how passive or aggressive you are in relation to your customer and client, and attenuate your attitude in order to help your prospect move into either an extroverted or introverted attitude to best fit the stage of the sale.

2. To gain trust whenever you approach another person, display open gestures and show the palms of your hands in the TruthPlane.
3. To build good rapport, find ways to sit or stand that do not put large barriers between you and others, block exits, or cause you to overshadow others with your height.

Theory to Practice

When it comes to "big versus small," perspective makes a difference, and it is easy to change physical position or perspective, and by doing so, change the brain's perception and functioning. Try this on for size: sit in a chair and get someone to stand close and over you to maximize the height difference. Next, ask this person to reprimand you as loudly and forcefully as possible. Then change positions: you stand up while your colleague sits and reprimands you from the chair.

You'll find that not only will your colleague find it nearly impossible to do this, but his voice will sound different and lack any authority. Of course, this is unusual (and could look kind of silly at the office), but it will give you a sense of how well you listened to your reprimand and the attitude it produced in you when you were being height-dominated. Did you notice your fight-or-flight mechanism kicking in? Try repeating the same exercise with your colleague at different levels of sitting, standing, and even lying down. When someone is lying down, the difference will be far more pronounced—you won't take the reprimand seriously at all.

C. S. Lewis, author of *The Chronicles of Narnia*, once said, "Enemy occupied territory is what the world is." How is someone invading your territory? And how might you be mirroring this behavior? Do you ever accidentally walk through a doorway and invade your clients' land? What do you see them doing in return—fight or flight?

A Body of Knowledge

Bruce Van Ryn-Bocking (thereptilianbrainatwork.com/blog) is an expert in human behavior in the workplace. He writes about the neuroscience of workplace relationships and workplace performance. Here he talks about a simple way to act around others to help you quickly get the best start on any sales relationship.

Open Hearts and Minds

Every person in love knows when their lover's heart is open and when it is closed. A closed heart usually precipitates the question, "What's wrong?"

Of course, when we speak about open and closed "hearts," we are talking about the limbic system—a part of our brain that takes a pivotal role in mediating emotions and relationships, and compels us to raise our young, live in families and villages, work and play together.

All human beings (except those with some sort of brain dysfunction) have the innate ability to know when another's heart is open or closed. This is because we are "tribal" in nature, and staying tuned to the mood of the alpha male or female is essential to staying in the tribe (and therefore to our survival).

I'm sure that your own personal experience will have shown that not only is it more pleasurable to have a conversation with an open-hearted person, but that you are much more likely to do business with that person than with a person who is either indifferent to you or who is closed.

The problem is that hearts open and close—depending on the weather, time of day, level of stress, anxiety about monthly sales targets, previous experiences, amount of sleep, etc.

Therein lays the problem for us salespeople—whenever I meet up with a potential client, my heart can be at either end of the "open/closed" spectrum. And the prospect will know this intuitively, before I even open my mouth.

So—what to do about this?

My goal is to have an open heart whenever I engage with a client or prospective client, or even someone whom I have no idea might ever become a client (a best friend or sister-in-law might be a potential client). Besides, I think it is the right thing to do!

How to do this? Here are three tips that might work for you:

1. Develop the ability to know whether your heart is open or closed. Ask friends and family if they think your heart is open or closed, and check against your self-perception. Also, notice when you are full of self-criticism. Chances are those are days when your heart is closed.
2. Develop the ability to open your heart intentionally. Most of us just do this unconsciously, and don't know how we did it. Set a goal to do this. Practice doing it (practice makes perfect).
3. When all else fails, pretend that your heart is open (fake it to make it).

Opening your heart to others can mean that their reptilian brain puts you in their "friend" category. That's the sweet place for doing business.

4

A Tribal Bazaar

Culture, Connection, Carnival, and Closing

Whenever it was feasible, I prefer to eat the rude.
—Dr. Hannibal Lecter

In this chapter you'll learn:

- Body language to connect you with the team
- The science of "pack mentality"
- Sales dress sense
- Tactics for managing yourself within an elite crowd
- Signals that attract a "predator" to you as a "victim"

Call it a clan, a gang, a network, a family, or call it a company: whatever you call it, whoever you are, tribes are everywhere. Groups, companies, departments, teams, markets, professional disciplines, and anywhere people with a common purpose or common experience gather, tribal behaviors will certainly be seen.

Identifying the tribe or tribes you are working with and understanding and accepting their behaviors can be essential to winning the sale. This is because every tribe has rules around how members behave and interact. Every tribe has some shared values, beliefs, rituals, customs, goals, concerns, and signals that drive how they perform. This behavior can also display the relative rank or social status of each member, and help you understand the influence each member may have. As a salesperson, you must find a way to work within the rules, hierarchy, and behavior to ensure you reach a status that will allow you to have respect and influence within the tribe for at least a short time—and in some cases the rest of your professional and even personal life.

A Taste for the Tribe

As an outsider, when the members of the tribe trust that you are aligned with their social order, you can be awarded the necessary status to participate in their decision making. Lose that trust and things can turn out pretty badly for you. Just look at the number of sales professionals who have exited the meeting room in which they just pitched, got straight on the phone to their sales manager and cried, "I GOT EATEN ALIVE IN THERE!"

Now, the last *actual* recorded cases of tribal cannibalism were during 1976, in the Jayawijaya Mountains in the Central Highlands region of Indonesian Papua New Guinea, where four Dutch missionaries were killed and eaten by the aboriginal Kombai tribespeople. It allegedly happened because the Dutch priest and his 12 companions tried to ban the locals from the indigenous customs (judged by missionaries as "pagan"), and they destroyed by fire some of the tribe's precious ritual items. Their intolerance for Kombai rituals and customs likely communicated a disregard and disrespect for their beliefs and values and so caused the ironic tragedy of the Dutch Christians ultimately ending up as the sacrificial lamb on the dinner table.

The key in sales is to be invited to sit around the dinner table and be part of the company—not be the actual meal itself! The word "company" is etymologically linked to the Latin *con panis*—"with bread" or "to break bread together." As the saying goes, "Families that eat together, stay together," and many companies are still family enterprises. You may well be selling to some of them. And a group of disparate shareholders often work on instilling corporate values for everyone to live by as a "corporate family." Think about that word "corporate," which means "to be united in one body." It is the job of the long-term sales professional to be invited into that united body, cooperate within the corporation, and celebrate with them in the provisions that are collectively brought to the table: to join the carnival and eat the feast!

Second Sitting

Let's take a moment to think about food, family, and company. Chances are you have already eaten at least once today—or if not, you will before too long. For many of us in a first world country, most of the time eating is a daily event that is so routine it is taken for granted. For many families, resources are abundant, and for others they are sometimes scarce. Some families buy what they want when they want; others must carefully plan how to get by day to day. However, there is no escaping the biological necessity for food. Everyone has to eat something—more or less nutritious and more or less regularly, whether you are going to purchase it in advance or on a leaner basis—as and when you need it.

Because the simple act of eating is essential to our biological survival, it is also extraordinary for its endless culinary forms and the cultural manners that go with it. This makes it a central part of cultural rituals designed to bond and deepen social relationships. Eating in a family is both a symbolic and a physical necessity. Across culture and time, food sharing is an almost universal medium for expressing such things as fellowship, hospitality, duty, gratitude, sacrifice, and compassion. Eating together is a universal symbol of trust and interdependency.

Thus, the physical imperative of eating when directed into a shared meal can be an enormous opportunity to display your nonverbal alignment to the goals, values, beliefs, rituals, customs, concerns, and signals of the tribe at whose "corporate table" (lean or opulent) you wish to be invited, graciously included, and accepted at.

Yet often you find it to be an exclusive meeting.

Sticky Toffee Puddings

Consider for a moment being in a sales call with two other people, both from a tribe different from yours. Imagine if this tribe was the Alumni of England's Cambridge University. But one of the two people is your sales partner on the sales call, and the other is the buyer.

The two Cambridge tribe members quickly and easily slide into the tribal ritual of status placement. They share the names of common contacts, perhaps other classmates and professors. They share the dates of their attendance and domain disciplines. Very quickly they position each other within the hierarchy of their tribe and establish a rapport that can support their sales conversation. They have formed their foundation of trust. Wonderful, but what about you? You did not, in this case, attend Cambridge, but a top university in another country. So while the other two are connected, how can you gain temporary status in the tribe to participate credibly in the conversation? They may not make it easy for you, as they simply may not recognize that you are being unconsciously placed as an outsider to their clique, with your sales partner unwittingly bringing down the strength of your own sales team.

Other tribal scenarios that you may recognize play out in selling situations across the world include: a software salesperson selling to partners in a law firm, a junior salesperson on a call with his boss, a young female salesperson presenting to a room full of middle-aged male executives. The context and circumstances are different from the example above, but the goal of gaining temporary status in the tribe to be able to hold your own, and even lead the sales process, can be a persistent challenge. So how can we get a handle on the culture of the tribe from the physical behavior of that group and work our way in?

Influence: Go with the Flow

Rituals and customs can be simple to detect because often by their very nature they are more physically based. What is the ritual of having a meeting? Is it like some of the U.S. big box stores or some Japanese manufacturing corporations where there may be a group chant beforehand? Who ritually sits where? Is it acceptable custom to leave the meeting table and walk around? How do others address each other or display that they would like to talk and add a point or ask a question?

The key here is to observe behaviors and show accepting body language around them—open gestures, listening, gently smiling, and gentle nodding of the head. You don't have to join in with the customs and rituals, and you certainly don't have to join in any that would make you feel *very* uncomfortable, but you do need to show that you *accept their behavior*. The wrong gesture of surprise, fear, disgust or, perhaps worst of all, disdain at the behavior of a group to which you are looking to establish a good relationship can get you "eaten" in the meeting for coming across as rude in the eyes of the group. The members of the tribe may not consciously understand why they now have feelings of aggression and animosity toward you. But you will certainly leave with the feeling that you are not wanted and have been "seen off" by them.

So take great care to keep yourself solidly in the center of the Door-Plane and in the TruthPlane while any behaviors that may feel alien to you are being played out. That way you stand a chance of appearing non-judgmental while internally you may still be screaming, "WHAT IS GOING ON HERE?"

A–Ω

Values are more difficult to pick up in the behavior of others, but of course you can look out for the way individuals share the valued resources within the hierarchy, and make sure that *you* respect that too. You may find that the "alpha" person in the group is given more space and more time. You may find that alphas take up a lot of territory, a lot of real estate in terms of both time and space. Alphas tend to gravitate toward the ends of the table, the positions of control with easy lines of sight to everyone else and important resources.

An alpha will often not be found sitting with her back to the door, for instance. And somewhat like a wolf pack, the rank order is maintained through ritualized posturing within the environment. Psychological warfare is preferable to physical confrontation, meaning that high-ranking status is based more on personality or attitude than on size or physical strength. And just like a wolf pack, there are those at the bottom of the pecking order—the omegas who can be used to absorb aggression from the rest of the pack and keep the relations between alphas and betas stable.

Unfortunately, sales reps can often be invited into the den to act as an omega—a kind of punching bag or kicking post upon which the alpha and betas can safely exercise their aggression with each other—and then send packing. You probably don't want to do this more than once with the same gang! However, another way to look at it is that when you have this position, you are at least in the tribe, just very low down in its ranks. Now comes the job of working your way up to beta level.

Watch out for how people physically greet each other and present themselves. Alphas assert their presence and tend to stand straight. Others in the hierarchy will adjust their positions to try to keep the alpha in front of the DoorPlane and stable. They will never want to drive them onto the back foot either physically or metaphorically unless they are making a play for the alpha position. They will never turn their back on an alpha unless by accident or because something else is happening in the environment that threatens the social order.

Observe and "mirror" (subtly copy) the behavior of the others in the group as far as it helps your positive relations with the decision makers, but also be conscious of the rank at which you are hoping to fit in within the hierarchy. Be respectful of the others in the room, but do not be afraid to assert yourself with body language that hints at the rank you believe you should be awarded. Take territory if you feel you need it to function at your best—give territory if you feel others need it to function at their best.

Affiliations to Appearance

Picture the following male sales professionals all selling the same service, and ask yourself whom you would trust to give you the most factual information when selling you a complex service:

- The casual guy with beard and open-necked shirt
- The lean, smooth, designer-glasses and all-in-black type
- The businesslike, short-haired, serious suit-and-tie
- Silver-haired man-in-a-jacket, softer, more friendly

Isn't the first consideration what they say and the strength of their evidence, rather than how they look? Maybe not? Because we treat people's appearance as a clue to their values. We expect the "Suit," for example, to be a person who thinks people should stand on their own feet. "Beard" believes in more equality. The designer type is a cool individualist. And the older guy defends tradition. These types are of course crude generalizations, but adapted roughly to those used by researchers at Yale University's cultural cognition research project. Moreover, it turns out that in tests, the Suits like to receive their information from like-minded Suits, and bearded gentlemen from like-minded men in beards, and so on. What cultural cognition means is that people form perceptions about the facts mostly in line with their existing values and cultural types—of which appearance is one part.

The reason people generally react in a close-minded way to new information is the risk that the implications of it may threaten them. So when the implication of some data affirms your values, you think about it in a much more open-minded way. Therefore, when it comes to agreement, how we identify with people is often more important to us than the facts they have to share. We trust whomever we identify as most likely to share our values and thus be less of a risk to us. And of course the way we dress and groom, the behavior we display, are the signals of the tribe with which we should be identified. We like the people who are like us, and we like the products and services from people we like! "Liking" is a major component of intimacy and bonding. The quicker we can get a client to like us, potentially the quicker we can move to the close.

Like other social mammals—wolves, whales, and apes, to name just three—we humans have an architecture in our brain that facilitates these tribal behaviors. And a knowledge of how it functions can help us understand how to use tribal instincts to our advantage.

Limbic Theory

Throughout its evolution, the human brain has acquired three components that progressively appeared and became superimposed, just like in an archeological site: the oldest, located underneath and to the back; the next one, resting on an intermediate position; and the most recent, situated on top and to the front. They are, respectively:

1. The *archipallium*, or primitive brain, which we have talked about in earlier chapters, comprising the structures of the brain stem—medulla, pons, cerebellum, mesencephalon, the oldest basal nuclei—the *Globus pallidus*, and the olfactory bulbs. It corresponds to the reptile brain, also called "R-Complex" by the senior research scientist at the American National Institute of Mental Health, Paul MacLean, who in 1973 proposed the Triune Brain model (Figure 4.1), where the brain can be categorized into three subdivisions corresponding to three consecutive evolutionary eras: the reptilian, the limbic, and the neocortical.
2. The *paleopallium*, or intermediate brain, comprising the structures of the limbic system. It corresponds to the brain of other mammals too and is essential to social behaviors.
3. The neopallium, also known as the superior or rational brain, comprises almost the whole of the hemispheres of the neocortex and some subcortical neuronal groups. It corresponds to the brain of the mammals, including the primates and, consequently, the human species.

According to MacLean, they are three biological "computers," which although interconnected, have retained, each one, "their peculiar types of intelligence, subjectivity, sense of time and space, memory, mobility, and other less specific functions."

The primitive (reptilian) brain, we know, is responsible for instinctual self-preservation. It is there that the mechanisms of aggression, repetitive behavior, and instincts for approach, attack, flight, feeding, mating, and the involuntary actions indispensable to the preservation of life are developed.

The limbic system (from the Latin word *limbus*, which implies the idea of a circle, since it forms a kind of border around the brain stem) commands certain social behaviors that are necessary for the survival of all mammals. Here, specific affective functions are developed, such as the one that induces mammals to nurse and protect their young, and develop ludic behaviors (playful moods). Some would say that subtle emotions and feelings beyond the reptilian reactions of good/bad—approach/avoid, like joy, sadness, and disdain, to name but a few, are developments originated in the limbic system. This system is also responsible for some aspects of personal and group identity.

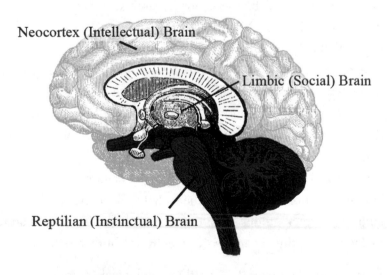

Neocortex (Intellectual) Brain

Limbic (Social) Brain

Reptilian (Instinctual) Brain

Figure 4.1 The Triune Brain

The third cerebral unit and final development is the neocortex or rational brain—a highly complex net of neural cells capable of producing a symbolic language, thus enabling humans to exercise skillful intellectual tasks such as reading, writing, and performing mathematical calculations—the mother of all invention.

Ancestral Advantage

This evolutionary perspective brings some clarity to behavior. Early vertebrates, having only what is now our brain core, optimized their survival in a variable environment with the sole use of instincts for finding, killing, and ingesting fuel, energy sources, avoiding others that would find, kill, and ingest *them* as fuel, and finally reproducing their genetic code. However, some animals survived better in their ecological niche by forming cooperative groups rather than competing individually.

Within the cooperating group, new social interaction properties that had evolved from genetic mutation caused the organisms to be fitter for the niche and so to stand more of a chance of passing on their genetic instruction to *be social* and have the brain to be social to the next generation (survival of the fittest). Antisocial behaviors were superseded by a completely different new set of survival optimizing social behaviors among allies—so tribal behavior, some might say, is more "evolved" behavior.

However, under immediate threat of danger and under extreme conditions, the social behaviors of the limbic brain are not appropriate, while those of the reptilian brain are more likely lifesaving. The reptilian brain can therefore gain instinctual executive function when under threat, stress, or duress. Hence, under the right conditions, the most social of us revert to antisocial behaviors! And that includes *you* and your customers.

Finally in our brain's evolution, with the arrival of the bilateral cerebral cortex, unwieldy chunks of multisensory cerebellar primary memory can be greatly reduced in size and converted into abstract summaries. Thus, abstract reasoning permits the reductive transformation and manipulation of complex information into a format that the mind easily manipulates.

What that last bit of waffle really means is that you can hold your past tucked away in your mind as memories—compressed data, if you will. And then pull them out and unpack them to predict your future through imaginary scenarios played out in your imagination. The benefit: this permits the evaluation of survival problems and their solutions by the safe production of imaginary trials, and their imaginary survival outcomes based on past experiences. It has also led to the development of abstract forms of communication called language and mathematics and this book, for example.

From these bases came a new form of self-awareness in us humans. This intellect sits high and mighty above the earlier reptilian and social executive brain instincts, intuition, and judgment. Yet again, under stress we can lose control of our individual intellectual function to our collective tribal and primitive behaviors. This means the lofty concept of the new technology of a better mousetrap that you are selling may not be heard by potential buyers and their tribe if you put pressure on the values they already hold dear as a group concerning mousetraps (in order to survive but not excel—remember, "evolution is lazy," it does just the minimum to survive). And the more you push the idea onto them, the more stress they feel, until they resort to reptilian brain thinking and you get eaten! The key to getting through is to always start your pitch by displaying an *acceptance* of their tribal values, which can be as easy as wearing the "national costume."

Tribal Dress Codes

In many societies and throughout history, people of high rank have reserved special items of clothing or decoration for themselves as symbols of their social status. Only Roman senators could wear garments dyed with Tyrian purple; only high-ranking Hawaiian chiefs could wear feather cloaks; and in China before the establishment of the republic, it is reputed that only the emperor could wear yellow.

Military, police, and firefighters often wear uniforms, as do workers in many other services and industries. Schoolchildren often wear school uniforms, while college and university students sometimes wear academic dress. Members of religious orders may wear uniforms. Sometimes a single item of clothing or a single accessory can declare one's occupation or rank within a profession.

Dress can symbolize a movement from one state to another (home to work and vice versa). It can show allegiance to a group, and the status, duties, and entitlements therein. It can protect against harm; it can create a hygiene barrier either physically (in the case or doctors) or metaphysically (in the case of priests). All in all, the way we dress has a profound psychological effect not only on those around us, but on us too.

Ethnocentric

In many regions of the world and across time, national costumes and styles in clothing and ornamentation declare membership in a certain village, caste, religion, etc. A Scotsman may traditionally declare his clan with his tartan (though most kilts seem to be worn at weddings by lowlanders looking for a romantic affiliation to a tribe for a day—and the opportunity to wear a knife in their sock without being arrested). A French peasant woman identifies her village with her cap or coif. A Palestinian woman identifies her village with the pattern of embroidery on her dress. Clothes can also proclaim dissent from cultural norms and mainstream beliefs, as well as personal independence. In nineteenth-century Europe, artists and writers lived *la vie de Bohème* and dressed to shock: female emancipationists wore bloomers, male artists wore velvet waistcoats and gaudy neck cloths. Bohemians, beatniks, hippies, Goths, Punks, Skinheads, Emos, and Little Monsters have continued the tradition in the twenty-first century.

In Tonga it is illegal for men to appear in public without a shirt, whereas on the nudist beaches of Saint Tropez it is totally fine if not a little over-dressed. In New Guinea and Vanuatu there are areas where it is customary for the men to wear nothing but penis sheaths in public—whereas this is uncommon and considered quite out of the ordinary on both Wall Street and Western Main Streets. Private organizations may insist on particular dress codes or standards in particular situations. Hierarchical management styles of the past that have shifted to more egalitarian flatter organizations may signal this with a more relaxed "casual Friday" dress code. Religious bodies may insist on their standards of modesty being maintained at their premises and events.

The Laws of the Land

And so to business and sales: employees are sometimes required to wear a uniform or to conform to certain standards of dress, such as a business suit or tie, because they need to appeal to a certain type of customer.

In the recent remake of the movie *The Adjustment Bureau* with Matt Damon (2011), Matt Damon's character, David Norris, in a confession during his election-losing speech, takes off his dress shoe and holds it up to the audience, explaining that his handlers have determined that his shoes cannot be so polished and shiny that he looks like a banker and turns off the common voter. At the same time they cannot be too scuffed or he will turn off the bankers as voters. The tone of the movie is that this is disingenuous somehow, but the reality is, as salespeople we are all making sure our shoes are "just right" in order to be accepted as a trustworthy guest member of the tribe. It matters: we just tend to dislike it when someone points it out to us, or judgmentally puts it into woolly contexts like "authenticity" or "being true to yourself."

White collar workplace clothing has changed significantly through the years. In the general corporate office, appropriate clothes are clean and business casual (dress shirt, polo shirt, trousers, skirts, etc.). Suits, neckties, and other formal wear are usually only appropriate in law offices and financial sector offices. Previous business dress code eras (the 1950s in the United States) featured standardized business clothes that strongly differentiated what was acceptable and unacceptable for men and women to wear while working. Today, the two styles have merged; women's work clothes expanded to include the suit (and its variants) in addition to the usual dresses, skirts, pants, and blouses; men's clothes have expanded to include bright colors and flamboyance.

Casual wear on the job entered the business world with the advent of a much more relaxed clothing expectation that came with the "Silicon Valley Tech" culture. Additionally, some companies set aside days—generally Fridays ("dress-down Friday," "casual Friday")—when workers may wear casual clothes. This practice has moderated somewhat since the end of the "dot-com" era. The clothing a company requires its workers to wear on the job varies with the occupation and profession.

The Casual Crowd

Business casual dress, also "smart casual," is a popular workplace dress code that emerged in white-collar workplaces in Western countries in the 1990s, especially in the United States and Canada. Many information technology businesses in Silicon Valley along with creative shops and media houses were early adopters of this dress code. In contrast to formal business wear, such as suits and neckties (the international standard business attire), the business casual dress code has no generally accepted definition; and its interpretation differs widely among organizations and is often a cause of sartorial confusion among the tribal members.

In general, business casual means dressing professionally, looking relaxed yet neat and pulled together. A more pragmatic definition is that business casual dress is the mid ground between formal business clothes and street clothes. Examples of clothing combinations considered appropriate for work by businesses that follow the business casual dress code is: for men, a shirt with a collar (polo shirt) and cotton trousers (or "khakis"); for women, a tennis shirt and trousers. Generally, neckties are excluded from business casual dress, unless worn in nontraditional ways. The acceptability of blue jeans and denim clothing varies—some businesses consider them sloppy.

As to knowing exactly how to fit in with a tribe by fitting in with the dress code, it's simple: hang out just at the edges of the tribe's territory and see what the members wear. Move your wardrobe further toward the clothes worn by others in their environment. A good rule of thumb for a salesperson is to dress within one style notch of the tribe. If meeting with the frontline teams that tend to be business casual, say a polo shirt and khakis, put on a jacket to present yourself with just a little more gravitas, but not so much that you look out of place. If meeting with executives who wear suits but their teams are casual, then a jacket and tie combination could be fine. If the entire environment is in suits, then it is time for a suit too, or at least a blazer and tie, but you cannot get away with the absent-minded professor look here—save it for Harvard!

The goal is the same as those of the (fictional) handlers of Matt Damon's David Norris character—be close enough to the range to not disrupt people's cognitive ease in seeing you. If you don't feel comfortable with wearing what they wear or you make a mistake and show up too far removed or missing a meaningful detail, then use your body language to show acceptance of their dress and to demonstrate your ease with the situation. Again, avoid looks of disdain, surprise, and disgust—from yourself and others around you—not to mention looks of fear when you encounter some piercings that look ever so painful. Always concentrate on being centered in the DoorPlane and open in the TruthPlane, and you may just get out alive!

Chapter 4 Quick Study

Even in a metropolis people work in "villages" or "tribes" that hold certain values they live by and that you must recognize if you wish to sell to them. The company values that are communicated on a website or via posters on the company walls are rarely the *real* "unspoken" values of the tribe. The unspoken values may be embodied within "rules," and sometimes the rules will create an environment that causes or determines some of the underlying values. Often the rules are embodied in the policies and procedures that one is asked to adhere to and are even enforced within the company. It is worthwhile for a salesperson to acknowledge these rules and embody them along with the tribe, because these rules will speak to their values.

As a rule of thumb, observe the behaviors of the tribe and show acceptance of those behaviors with using open body language. This way you don't necessarily need to join in (it may not fit your values), but you can show that you are not disrespectful of others who have a different value system.

Just Do This Now

1. When meeting a new group of buyers, slow down a little and take your time to watch, listen, and mirror the behaviors that people show in the team you wish to become part of, dressing appropriately for that tribe.
2. When behaviors push against your own values, make a conscious effort to keep yourself physically centered in the DoorPlane and gesturing in the TruthPlane to keep your own reptilian brain from getting triggered to fight or flight.
3. Show curiosity in the customs of the group, and where possible, join in on the ones that involve food. For example: if they like to get coffee from the mom and pop shop on the corner, now is not the time to turn your nose up and say, "I only drink Starbucks!" Either join them gracefully or say you've had your dose of caffeine already, thanks.

Theory to Practice

The great individualist anarchist Henry David Thoreau said: "It is an interesting question how far men would retain their relative rank if they were divested of their clothes." Let's test that idea.

Dress up to go to the grocery store or a hardware store on a Saturday. The grocery store is probably somewhere you do not think to dress up, but if you show up on Saturday in your best clothes, watch how people react to you, especially the people working in the store. You will see that they treat you differently. Keep your body language in the TruthPlane and see what happens.

In the hardware store that difference may not command the same level of respect. You will look out of place; they will struggle to imagine you under your sink fixing that link. Combine this circumstance with body language in the PassionPlane, and in all likelihood the clerk will struggle to put up with you. You just will not fit with the sensibilities of the tribe.

Try the opposite: dress way down and then visit a high-end store. *If* they let you in, you will likely see a difference. They may be well-trained salespeople, but watch their body language to see how they react to your status. Now in this instance keep your body language in the GrotesquePlane; you might struggle to even get service.

Psychological phenomena are not just things that happen "inside" us, but what happens in relation to us—between us and our environments—and hence they are ecological. Our psychology is a response and a provocation to the environment around us, including the groups of humans we feel ourselves part of or not part of.

A Body of Knowledge

Tracey Thomson is an entrepreneurial consultant who helps companies grow through solid business development. Tracey is a driving force at TruthPlane (truthplane.com), managing and steering the company alongside Mark Bowden. Tracey's background in entertainment led her to develop her own production company, creating a variety of entertainment concepts for theater and TV. Here, she talks about performing to fit in and get ahead with some exclusive foreign tribes.

Old-Skool Tie

In my early days as a North American woman working in the UK, I was automatically an outsider. In every meeting, I felt I was fighting to rise up from a lower status and prove myself.

This outsider status peaked while I was working with a London-based consultant as the business development expert. The consultant in question had brought me in to help launch an exciting new venture; and so, working through her well-established and phenomenal network of industry leaders in London, we were pitching this fresh opportunity for financial support.

Despite all best efforts by my trusted and well-connected consultant companion to champion my talents and respectability to our potential business partners, it seemed that I inspired their suspicion or, worse, indifference; it became apparent that in their eyes I might be more suitably placed staying quiet and taking notes, or perhaps fetching coffee.

After recovering from the shock, rage, and irritation brought on by the multitude of obvious slights coming my way—one high profile head of an important industry association refused to look at me to the point of keeping his entire body turned away from me for an entire two-hour meeting where there were only three of us in the room(!), addressing only my companion—I began to examine more closely what was actually going on.

My colleague shared a similar background to the people in her network, understood the same cultural references, sometimes had attended the same schools, knew many of the same people—in other words, she came from the same tribe. I had none of this mutual background to fall back on.

As my concern over my lack of status grew, so did more aggressive attempts to reverse this problem, which made it exponentially worse—I was nervously (and unknowingly) fidgeting, talking too much and too loudly, smiling enthusiastically at every opportunity, leaning toward the people in the meeting to the point of lurching over the table . . . increasingly erratic behavior in meetings that was not helping inspire trust and acceptance; or in other words, crazy and desperate was clearly not the way to sell!

I had to figure out a way I could instantly establish myself somewhere in their field of understanding that inspired their trust (so I could effectively get to the business at hand), or at the very least so they wouldn't see me as a threat or simply a nonentity. I became awesome at effectively using my body language to show I was listening. I would sit calmly in my chair so that people could clearly see me across a table, avoid any fidgeting, never rest my head in my hands, so that all was visible; I encouraged my companion to tone down any desires to gush about my talents in the meetings. Rather, we would focus on painting the picture of being a solid and trustworthy team that had every angle covered, so that with our intelligence, energy, and their resources we could and would nail this new business venture, ensuring success for everyone.

And it worked!

Ivor Benjamin is a stage director and chair of the Directors Guild of Great Britain. For over two decades he has been teaching Stage-Fight 101 to young actors and directors, and he has a wealth of knowledge on how actors should move in order to influence any audience, at a primal level, into feeling that real violence has occurred on the stage. Here he talks about the body language of "the victim" and how to avoid it in the sales situation.

You Talking to Me?

Stage-fighting is, of course, the opposite of real combat—it's more like a mime or dance. "Fighters" work together to create the illusion of violence—otherwise there would never be a second night or a second take. Most performers pick it up right away, but once in a while you find an actor who can't figure out how to mime a push, a slap, or a blow and does it for real! Oddly enough, though, it is often "the victim" who initiates this real violence in the way they look at their partner.

When someone feels they are being victimized, they find it very hard to look their opponent in the eyes. Often, failing to meet an attacker's gaze results in a quick glance at the assailant and then an equally quick look away—something known as "the victim flick." Not only does this eye-flick signal to an attacker that their victim is afraid—it triggers a deeper response, increasing aggression and creating an inevitable vicious circle of "predator and prey" that can end in real violence.

Breaking that response is usually as simple as asking the victim to maintain steady eye contact—which is part of the technique of stage-fight anyway.

This done, attackers who are tricked into real aggression by the visible fear of their partner quickly resume their role as an equal partner in the "dance."

5

Realizing Relationships
in Sales

Pleasure, Utility, and Virtue

*I present myself to you in a form suitable to the relationship
I wish to achieve with you.*

—Luigi Pirandello

In this chapter you'll learn:

- The levels of relationship you can build as a sales professional
- How to take the heat off of you under criticism
- Setups for cooling down the conflict at sales meetings
- The body language of the consultant, coach, and trusted advisor
- Goals and gestures when selling to life partners

The ancient philosopher Aristotle classified relationships into three types:

1. **Relationship of Pleasure.** This is are when you find a partner who's all about giving you a physical experience. It's about nurturing the body and senses—nothing very deep or long term.

    The problem is with purely selling to pleasure in a situation where you want the customers to come back again: if they were unhappy or not completely satisfied on the physical experience level with you the first time, they are likely to go elsewhere next time. It is a purely transactional relationship. Worse still, they may warn their friends not to buy from you either. But if it was good, then they may be back to create what Aristotle would probably have called a . . .

2. **Relationship of Utility.** This can be longer term, but only if relating with you brings social and personal status and power to the buyers. To put it coolly or quite simply, they are using you to inflame their egos on a more regular basis (and they may well do the same for you). That may look like stereotypical rich partner/trophy partner "sold mates"—rather than soul mates.

    With utility comes a great experience with the product or service, and increased power and social cachet. If the person is going to buy often, the relationship may need to develop into a genuine friendship. As Aristotle might say, a . . .

3. **Relationship of Shared Virtue.** This relationship makes both of you better people. It makes you ascend to a level above physical resource, power, and social cachet. There is challenge, learning, and the opportunity to maximize potential on many levels for both partners. The best sales relationships (long-term, repeat sales in many cases), and the "trusted advisor" status many sales professionals seek, are built on a relationship of shared virtue.

This chapter will show you how to use your nonverbal communication to create an environment that signals your intent to build a relationship of shared virtue and what many call "Consultative Selling."

Win/Win

Aristotle also said that if you want to enjoy a thriving relationship built to last over the long haul, you must prioritize seeking a Relationship of Shared Virtue — instead of "superficial lures" and "material goods." He went on: "Men imagine the causes of happiness lie in external goods. That is as if they were to ascribe fine and beautiful lyre playing to the quality of the instrument rather than the skill of the player." So in the shared virtue model we admire the skill of the players on top of the goods or service they seek to provide. And whereas in one-off selling the buyer has the most to lose, in relationship selling, the seller can be the biggest loser if he sells something that is not wanted. Not only may the product be returned, but all future sales may be lost. Trust-building is such a major activity in this approach that it can take up to half of any sales professional's time.

The foundation of a shared virtue relationship is the aspiration for a win/win sales result. The seller wants the buyer to feel that he got a fair deal, and the buyer, although she wants a good price, does not want the seller to go out of business. Many negotiable things beyond price are on the table, including goodwill and future opportunities. Relationship selling happens in any place where, along with the transaction, relationships are important too. In the same way as when two life partners are negotiating something, they will be more successful if both consider the relationship as well as whatever it is they each want.

B2B

A typical place where such relationship selling takes place is in business-to-business (B2B) situations, and even more so where selling and buying are both professional activities and full-time salespeople deal with full-time buyers. When the smart buyer has been on a wide range of sales courses, she can often see selling techniques coming from a mile away.

However, this sales relationship is also important in retail or business-to-consumer (B2C) situations. While the relationship here, depending on the product line, may be a single transaction or an opportunity for multiple transactions over time, the seller will do well to present a win/win posture and aim to build a relationship of shared virtue. The focus of the salesperson is to help solve genuine problems that her customers are experiencing, and she often takes time to acquire a deep understanding about her customers' businesses, using methods such as *SPIN Selling, Customer-Centered Selling,* or *Consultative Selling.* The goal is to deliver value for both the seller and buyer.

Relationships Under Pressure

In practice, selling is a pressure-filled business. The salesperson must deliver results measured against his quota, as in the end he gets paid to close business deals, not make friends. In many cases the buyer is under just as much pressure. Buying the right thing, getting it for the right price and terms, and having it do the right things are all results of the purchase that the buyer will judge and be judged upon. In this pressurized environment it is easy for everyone to fall into bad habits, jeopardize trust, and miscommunicate. Effective use of the TruthPlane and its ability to keep you calm and clear-headed in the face of pressure will help you build the right kinds of relationships that actually help the salesperson deliver the required results, and help the buyer make good decisions even in the most aggressive of situations.

If there is a conflict, you may tend to find there is another human being involved, because on the whole it takes two or more to have an argument. When there is conflict around the product or service you are selling, it is often the case that you—the salesperson—end up becoming an avatar for that product or service—*you* feel attacked! And so you can easily start to feel negative toward your customer or client, and the relationship of shared virtue comes under pressure.

Although there is some positive effect in having a potential buyer vent his problems, frustrations, and anxieties around what you are selling him, there is also a downside in that he may now associate you with many of those potentially negative and damaging feelings. This is why it is often a great idea to create a third point of reference you can associate with the product and service—something more transactional: a model, a diagram, a brochure, ready-made pictures, or a quickly drawn representation on a whiteboard that can become the nonverbal focus for both of you to push problems, frustrations, and tough questions at. It is now far easier for you to side with your client, to totally accept his point of view, because that point of view is now not directed so aggressively toward you, but toward this third point.

Drawing Them In

Imagine an architect attempting to influence and persuade a potential client to buy into a radical new design for her building. Without any physical third point of reference, the client physically faces the architect full on and delivers all the issues around what for the architect may be some very personal work. The architect easily becomes defensive, frustrated, and even angry at the client. And because from the client's point of view she is "just being helpful" in advising what will best suit her needs, it is easy to assume from the nonverbal feedback that the architect maybe does not like her personally. In return, of course, the client starts to "mirror" and not like the architect. A potential breakdown in the relationship is unconsciously happening right in front of their eyes.

Now imagine that the architect quickly brings out a pad of paper and rough-sketches the design. He moves the paper over to the client, gives her his pen, and says, "Show me what isn't working quite right about this design." The client points to the sketch with her pen as both of them face this third point and move their energy and critical attitude in toward that instead of the designer. "I get it," says the architect. And gesturing again toward the diagram adds, "Sketch out now what would work better for you." The client scribbles out some possibilities. The architect takes out another pen and says, "Let me make some suggestions to that," and begins to add ideas to the client's suggestions on the paper.

Instead of conflict between the parties, both are now working together on the same solution, and all potential conflict is directed toward a third point of focus. As the client's body language opens up and displays a feeling of ease around the design, the architect moves the drawing farther toward his own body and territory, lifting it closer to the client's face in order to bring her back to face-to-face contact with him. He smiles and nods at the new idea, takes the diagram off to one side, and now engages the client directly again.

You can of course see how the third point of reference is a great nonverbal tool for persuasion and influence. But what happens when that third point is another person? And if that person is you? How can you nonverbally manage your relationship in the sale when you are the "third wheel"?

My Friend's Amazing

As we have discussed, the environment around you has a huge impact on how people perceive you, and of course how easily they trust you. The *peo-*

ple around you are part of your environment as well, and so the way they behave around you ultimately reflects on you and whether others can trust you or not. So how do you bring a new person into the sales process who may not have the credibility you have or may not have the same level of trust built with your client?

Well, of course you are part of your sales partner's environment, so you must present yourself in a form suitable to the relationship you wish to achieve between your client and your partner. And here's a way to do it: whenever your sales partner is speaking, presenting, or interacting with the client in any way, look at your partner and think to yourself, "My friend is amazing!" As your partner is talking to the client and you are thinking, "My friend is amazing," every now and then look back toward your client, and when you catch his eye, move your gaze back to your partner—again always thinking to yourself, "My friend is amazing!"

This powerful mantra causes your body language to become open and positive, and your client will mirror that feeling. As you constantly bring your gaze back to your sales partner, you will cause your client to mirror that movement and give his eye contact to your partner. This gives the new person in the relationship a good rank or status within the tribe you are forming together with the customer or client.

Now what happens when the tribe grows in size?

Them and Us

The number of people who are in a room together and how they are placed will have a definite bearing on how they relate to and engage with each other.

Notice how when two parties come to meet, they will often sit on opposite sides of a table. This is automatically adversarial in terms of the territory. There is now a "my side" and a "your side," with a large gulf in between. It is easy for this to happen, for groups to unconsciously sit on either side of a table together and so unwittingly set up an adversarial meeting of team versus team. Notice how parliaments are often deliberately set up in this aggressive manner, with the psychological barrier of a no-man's-land that people are traditionally banned from crossing (unless they are changing their allegiance, or "crossing the floor," as it is called). It is no surprise that the British prime minister Sir Winston Churchill once said, "We shape our buildings; thereafter they shape us." So the simple solution is always to take away the "architecture" that supports the conflict—remove the table.

But of course this sometimes has some negative consequences that call for other solutions. In this case, you can simply make a conscious effort to mix up the parties from both sides of the deal. Doing so quickly breaks down the power of the largest antagonistic marker in the space (the table) and discourages embedding in the attitude of "your side." You will be helping both groups see the other's point of view by placing them where they can literally get each other's perspective.

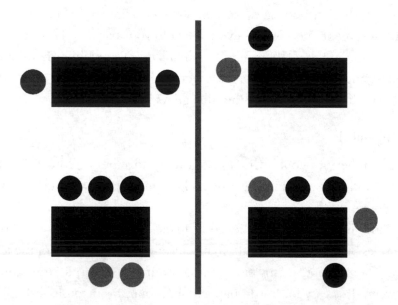

Figure 5.1   Confrontation Versus Collaboration

Which of the sales meetings in Figure 5.1 look the most collaborative and which the most confrontational if "black" is the buyer? What difference occurs if we make "gray" the buyer, and why?

One, Two, Three, Four, Lots

Remember, once a person sees more than four people at one time, that person's unconscious mind defines that number as a crowd (Figure 5.2). How intimidating it is, then, for someone to walk into a room with anything more than four people in it: "Oh, no, a gang!"

The solution to this problem is that if you wish to create an environment that is welcoming to potential clients or partners, you should organize your team in such a way that you break up the numbers of people grouped together so that your team is less intimidating when guests enter the meeting room. If you wish to be most inviting to a client entering a space, be sure that the people who are receiving the guest are grouped in twos or threes, rather than standing around looking like a big gang.

The more you control the environment, the greater your chance of being able to control the outcome of that meeting, investigation session,

Figure 5.2 Conspiracy Versus Consultancy

or negotiation. As always, the first step in determining how to lay out a meeting room is to consider your objective. When your goal is to generate creative thinking and lots of new ideas around the sale, then the layout of the room must work toward that.

Get Creative

A "living room style" room with chairs or couches could be more appropriate for a thinking session where a free flow of ideas is encouraged. The informality of such an arrangement invites playfulness and creativity. Perhaps the living room in a hotel suite is the best option in this case. But if you do not have the luxury of using a layout such as that, then place tables in a shallow U-shape so that as a facilitator you can write on flip charts that can be seen by everyone. Also, everyone should easily see and hear one another. Perhaps place the refreshment table in the room to the back or the side. This way, people can help themselves without leaving the room (because you know what leaving the room can become—a time to make or take a call, check in with the office, run into a colleague, and before you know it 20 minutes have passed without a key decision maker having been part of the process).

Have natural light if at all possible. A windowless room can make participants feel closed in. You don't want them to feel that way when you are looking for breakthroughs in their thinking! And certainly you don't want them to feel closed in during a negotiation where you need to open their minds to new ways of seeing the details of the deal—you will instead invite them to close their thinking down with an interrogation cell atmosphere!

We Have Ways of Making You Balk

The raw space in which you hold a negotiation can act to relax or press in on the negotiators. Generally, more space is better, although not so much space to bring on agoraphobia, or make people otherwise uncomfortable. Many negotiations have elements of confidentiality about them, and in such cases the room should feel appropriately private. When there are several people in the negotiation and they're sitting around a table, remember that they need space to get up and not feel squashed, which diminishes their rank and status. Looking for a relationship of partnership around the negotiation, you need to sit closer and to one side of the person you are looking to be aligned with. If you are negotiating within a group, then once again the long boardroom table setup, with opposing sides sitting to one side of each other in a "them and us" parliamentary type orientation, is potentially a recipe for discord. Try moving your negotiation to the private room of a Chinese restaurant, where traditionally the table is round and there is a culture of sharing. Be sure that team members are sitting next to your client's team members so that the idea of "them and us" is broken up as much as is possible under the circumstances.

Sometimes even just an empty space where people can stand—for example, when having coffee—is a useful addition. In moments when they are more relaxed and have some comfort and stimulation from not only the caffeine but also the increased circulation (not sitting on the largest muscle in the body anymore), they can be opened up further to the opportunities you have for them. When you change the physical position, you stand a good chance of shifting the psychological position also. If the negotiations meet an impasse, you can take the opportunity to move people's perceptual position and free up their minds by taking the opportunity to physically move to another position in the room. For instance, you can stand up and grab a coffee while inviting your client over for one too, and then continue the meeting negotiation standing together and consuming a resource, rather than sitting with nothing! At every opportunity find ways to collaborate in a physical activity to promote mental collaboration and agreement.

Are You Triadically Skilled?

When one person alerts another to a stimulus by means of eye-gazing, finger-pointing, or other verbal or nonverbal indication, this is known as "joint attention." When one person gazes at another person and then points to an object, and then returns her gaze back to the other person, this is "initiating joint attention." The person who looks toward the referenced object is "responding to joint attention." And joint attention is referred to as a "triadic skill," meaning it involves two people and an object or event outside of the duo. Behavioral scientists have noted the important and unique role that eye gaze plays in the primal behaviors of establishing dominance, initiating and terminating aggression, indicating the location of food, signaling the direction of an approaching predator, and also within mating behaviors. But what is so interesting about this for sales?

Although a triadic eye gaze can also be used to regulate one-to-one social interactions, another major and unique function of a triadic eye gaze is that it can be used to reveal an individual's focus of attention and internal state—his desires and goals—and that's why in sales there is a primal advantage to bringing your customer or client's attention to a third point between you: a sales brochure, diagram, or sample perhaps. Maybe even the product itself.

Learn to Listen

Of course, agreement through collaboration moves forward only when another trusts that you are a listener. Listening, especially active (purposeful) listening, is the habit of trustworthy people. When you actively listen, you are giving others your maximum attention. There is a great question to ask yourself when you communicate: "Am I listening or *reloading*?" Unfortunately, many in sales are not really listening; they are preparing for their next chance to speak. Buyers can sense this, and it erodes their trust in the sincerity of the relationship. We all know that as sales professionals closing is all important; but with that as a focus, it is easy to be consumed by your own dialogue toward that goal rather than what the client is saying. By effectively managing your "listening" posture, you can help keep yourself focused on the buyer and really listen to her moving forward.

So what does listening look like?

Exercise Your Ears

Let's try some deliberate listening and see what works. Turn on the radio, find some spoken word on the Internet, or maybe just switch on the TV and then turn your back on the picture to *just listen to the voices*. As you do this, drop your hands down by your sides and hold your head straight. How do you feel listening in this position? How engaged do you feel with the words that are spoken? How much time do you think you have to engage with what is being said? Do you feel relaxed, hurried, or is your mind simply shifting on to other more important things that have nothing to do with the words coming from the media? Perhaps these things are more related to you, rather than whatever the speaker is speaking about right now?

Keep on listening, but try another physical position. Bring your hands up to the TruthPlane. You can interlace your fingers gently, if you like, and just hold your palms facing your belly button. Or if you'd like to put more effort in, hold your hands open as you listen and gesture gently in toward yourself now and again, as if making the suggestion, "Tell me more." How does this feel to you? Carefully note any changes in your ability to listen from when your arms were down by your sides and you placed your hands in the TruthPlane. Are you feeling more engaged with what the speaker is saying? Do you feel you have more time to listen to whatever he is talking about? Would you rate this listening position as being better than in the first (hands down in GrotesquePlane) position?

Now let's add a further gesture to this: tilt your head gently to one side by about five to ten degrees. It's a very small movement. As you continue to listen to the speaker with your head tilted gently to one side, nod gently as you listen. Have your hands in the TruthPlane either gently interlaced over your belly button or making small gestures of the kind that signal you wish to get more from the speaker.

How do you feel as the listener here? Has your engagement with what is being said escalated? Do you feel quite engaged with what is being said? It stands to reason that if you are *feeling* more engaged as the listener, then you stand a very high chance of *looking* more engaged. And this looks and feels good to a client because there is very little that people enjoy more than the feeling that they're being listened to. To be listened to raises both your personal status and your rank within the tribe and so produces dopamine in the reward centers of the brain for a feel-good effect.

One last element to this exercise: as you gesture in the TruthPlane, your head gently tilted to one side and nodding as you listen, simply smile gently. How has this affected your overall appreciation and acceptance of what is being said? Do you now feel really good about what you heard? Do you feel that not only are you listening but that you accept and appreciate what you are listening to?

Again, if it feels like you are listening, accepting, and appreciating the content, it's highly likely that a client of yours would feel it too—would feel accepted and appreciated. In life, it is generally rare for others to feel listened to, accepted, and appreciated. If you make yourself into a sales professional who always listens to your customers and clients, accepts and appreciates what they have to say, you stand a greater chance of being a unique person in their eyes. You stand a great chance that they will want a relationship of shared virtue with you, rather than one of utility or pleasure. And so you also stand a better chance than many other people this client or customer comes into contact with (including sometimes his own family) that he will see you as a trusted advisor—not because you necessarily give advice, but because you actively listen. This gives you more credibility.

Dropping Off into the Grotesque

In nature there are only two reasons for you to drop your arms: to rest or to move. With your arms dropped and your adrenaline pumping, your weight will start to shift in front of an audience, literally making you look shifty and making it difficult for those watching you to trust you. This shifting can easily escalate into pacing up and down. The brain says that if we have our arms by our sides, we should be moving, especially with all those people looking at and judging us.

But when you stand still with your arms hanging down, the body takes this as a signal to rest, or even sleep. That is the biggest reason why the room can get sleepy in a sales presentation: you are standing still with your arms hanging down. The potential buyers quickly copy the leader and let their arms relax in their chairs, sit back, and trance out. They become the living dead, just like the presenter. With the arms hanging down and the body still, a person's heart rate, breathing rate, blood pressure, and levels of oxygen to the body and brain can decline quite rapidly, taking the brain's electrical activity to a state dangerously near the theta wave rhythmic cycle of sleep. The voice follows and drops significantly in tone (another nonverbal indicator of the meaning behind a message). This deeper voice then tends to drop even further at the end of each thought, and there are only three reasons for such a downward intonation: sleep, depression, and dormancy.

What do we mean by this?

If we look at the origin of the word "credibility," we find it derives from the late twelfth century Latin *credo* meaning "I believe." It is a feeling, an internal state. We project credibility onto others. So the question is, how do we persuade and influence others to have belief in *our* abilities and to join with us in a relationship of shared virtue—to let us be their trusted advisors? Because from this position, you can drive value-based sales conversations with the buyer efficiently; that is, with shorter sales cycles.

Way of the Dragon

Not only does your posture generally create a sense of credibility, but also the way you move that posture gives others a sense of your creed—what we should believe about you. This in turn can attract others to relate to you—or not. Of course, we know that the posture to use in order to deliver a sense of calm and assertiveness is open gestures around the navel area, that is, the TruthPlane. Keeping yourself just a little in front of the DoorPlane keeps you in a calm and assertive position—neither passive (way behind the door) nor aggressive (way in front of the door). Furthermore, stillness is an indicator of status within a social group, and therefore gives others the idea that you are calm and assertive.

So often we might try to get attention by moving around and making as much noise (be it sonic or visual) as possible to gain attention; but instead let's try to harness the power of stillness when we communicate.

Try this now: Think of a part of your sales process and get a moving picture in your mind about how you feel you move during that part of the process. In your mind watch yourself as if watching a film, and take notice of how you move. Listen to yourself speaking in this film, and take note of the quality of your speech, of its speed, tone, and cadence. Now pause that movement for a moment (don't stop breathing in this film of yourself, obviously!), press Play again on the you in the movie, and try to control your movements with more of a sense of "flow," avoiding sharp or staccato movements.

Notice how this affects your voice and the way you are able to think. Do you find that you stand or sit with a feeling of more power and status when your movement flows? Are you able to listen better to others? If so, remember how your customers and clients are designed to mirror your clearest and most consistent behavior. If you think you are able to absorb messages better in this state, imagine how your clients or customers who join you in this stillness will more fully absorb the impact of your message, and how they can be more adaptable, more able to change their minds.

In 150 BC a Chinese Taoist, Ho Shang Kung, said, "A dragon is still, hence it is able to constantly transform itself. A tiger is busy, hence it dies young." When calmness in the body replaces tension, anxiety often drifts away and the likes and dislikes, preferences and aversions, wants and don't wants—which can arise out of anxiety and cause conflict between you and others in relation to you—often begin to feel less significant. And of course, within the anxiety-producing environment of a sales process (anxiety producing because we never know for sure if the buyer will buy or back out), in an effort to reconcile this inner conflict it is all too easy to end up trying to manipulate and cajole the world and events in an aggressive manner to suit your own ends. It can end up as the proverbial "hitting your head against the wall." Instead of aggressive manipulation, try to be still and to accept the situations and relationships as they are right now, knowing that these things can change of their own accord.

So if and when aspects of the sale start to move chaotically (for any reasons, be they good or bad), try changing your thinking and actions to match whatever situations and relationships are *constant*. While a sales situation can get exciting with new ideas and details, often the excitement can build so much that the transaction as a whole goes off-track. (Trying to manage the smaller details can divert the course and put you into postures that put you at risk of losing the credibility you've worked hard to build.) A considered and powerful long-term reaction to the unpredictable can be a better strategy than constant hard changes, as on the tiller of a boat tossed across rough seas, where you force the journey against all odds. Stay centered when the relationships get tough, and be an image of calm water for everyone to gravitate and steer toward.

Chapter 5 Quick Study

Long-term, repeat sales and the "trusted advisor" status is the preferred state for many sales professionals. This relationship is one of *shared virtue*, where there is challenge, learning, and the opportunity to maximize potentials on many levels for both partners; or as some may call it, "win/win" or "Consultative Selling." Getting this status is not just about having the right product, service, gap, or consultative questions; it is also about showing up with the right attitude, being able to demonstrate physically that you listen, are engaged, can take and work with criticism and manage many sides and factions within the stakeholders present. Be adaptable, calm, and assertive when many around you may be stuck or simply losing their heads under the pressures of coming to the right solution.

Just Do This Now

1. Find ways to sit with a client so that the two of you are free from physical barriers, for example, at the corners of a table rather than across from each other, or in a lounge rather than a boardroom. Look for third points of reference to direct any aggression toward.
2. Adopt the physicality of "listening" rather than "telling," even if you are giving instruction, for example, open in the TruthPlane, head tilted to one side, gently nodding your head with a slight smile on your face.
3. Be quieter both in how much you speak compared to how much you listen, and how much you move. Bring the tempo of your movement

down and make your movement more direct, still, and flowing (adaptable like water) rather than indirect, abrupt, and staccato—like fire.

Theory to Practice

Are you generally a good listener or a bad listener? Who taught you how to listen? Anyone come to mind as your role model for the type of listening you generally do? How good would that role model be at your job today?

Think of someone who would be or already is brilliant at your job. Watch her to ascertain what behaviors she uses that show she is listening. Practice, mirror, or model those behaviors when you are next in a sale situation, and note what effect it has on the feeling of the relationship between you and your client or customer. You can even ask, "Do you feel that I have listened to all you need to tell me today?" and listen and work with the feedback.

A Body of Knowledge

Michael Bungay-Stanier is the senior partner at Box of Crayons (boxofcrayons.biz), a company that helps organizations do less Good Work and more Great Work. His most recent book, a collection of essays by thought leaders on Great Work, entitled *End Malaria*, raised more than $300,000 for Malaria No More. Here he talks about how the body language of a coach can help you guide your clients more easily toward a consultative sale.

Body Based Curiosity (It's Not as Kinky as It Sounds)

As a sales professional, it's tempting to think that coaching is just another word for giving people the advice they need.

Sure, perhaps you're doing it in a more caring-sharing way than old school command and control, but still it's clear that the expertise is flowing from you to them.

If you're a manager or leader, it's giving the guidance to your team to help them do better.

If you're in the field, it's helping your prospects see the light.

But if you want to be a powerful coach, and in doing so engage those with whom you're working in a more focused, deeper, and less transactional relationship, giving advice is the last thing you want to be doing.

The fundamental shift you need in your behavior is this: less advice, more questions.

Or to put it another way: less expert, more curiosity.

What's great is, you already know this.

You already know that question-based selling works much more effectively than advice-laden selling.

The tricky part of it all is that you also already know how tempting it is to slip into advice giving, solution-finding and answer-providing at the slightest invitation.

So how do you manage yourself better to resist the lure of advice and ask more questions?

The Change to Make

Let's assume your body has two states of being. One is the Expert Stance, and the other is the Coach Stance.

The Expert Stance is the position your body takes when you're giving advice.

Your job is to notice what your own Expert Stance is.

Mine? I'm sitting more forward and more upright in my chair. I'm wishing they'd be quiet so I could tell them what they need to know. I'm in my own head phrasing the persuasive point I have to make. My right foot might be tapping or twitching. My hands are tense. I'm nodding in a pseudolistening sort of way that really means hurry up and shut up.

Your Coach Stance is the way your body is when you're curious. You want to notice what this is for you too.

For me, it's sitting back in the chair, noticing the hypotheses and conclusions I'm drawing, but not acting on them. My hands are still and more relaxed. I might have my hand up on my chin, I'm breathing a little slower, and my feet are still and on the floor.

Your Body Leads Your Brain

We tend to assume that if we think a certain way, our body will follow along. But I think that if you strike a particular stance, your brain will follow your lead. So if you see the value of being more coachlike in the way you work, don't think about it. Rather, embody it. Put your attention on taking up your Coach Stance and maintaining it as best you can. You'll find yourself in a place of powerful curiosity rather than tiresome expertise.

Rona Birenbaum is a fee-for-service financial planner and the owner of Caring for Clients financial planning (caringforclients.com). She and her team provide independent, holistic financial advice that demonstrates care and provides peace of mind. She is a master in the communication strengths and the subtlety needed to help clients choose the best way forward for themselves financially.

And she's a genius at doing this with life partners. Here she talks about just that.

Is It Hot in Here or What?

When couples meet with me for the first time to discuss financial planning in general, and our services in particular, I never know whether the individuals are feeling aligned or in conflict.

Sometimes the conflict is clear right away. "He likes to spend on cars and computer stuff and doesn't care about saving for our future." Or "She doesn't appreciate how hard I am working. I'm doing my best." Or "He thinks I spend too much money on the children."

Other times it is more subtle. One person does all the talking, while their life partner stays silent, not agreeing or disagreeing with anything said. Until I ask them, "So, is that the way you see it?"

There Is Always Tension

There are few topics of conversation more sensitive than money. But there is always tension of one kind or another within the mind or heart of any prospective customer.

That's because there is rarely only one person involved in a purchase decision. Even when one individual has the final say on whether to purchase your product or service, there are always others who need to express their support either directly or indirectly.

What's Your Objective?

Be honest. Do you just want to make a sale? If so, you can simply ignore the tension and steamroll toward it. Or do you want to use the product that you sell or the service you provide to enhance people's lives (including your own)? That approach will define you as a valued supplier or trusted advisor over the long run.

Creating the Environment

My goals when meeting with clients in conflict are that they express themselves without fear of judgment, acknowledge each other's perspective, acknowledge shared values and goals, and agree to work together on those common goals.

To achieve this, I try to maintain a relaxed and open physical demeanor. It helps me keep my mind open and listening actively. I sit in my chair and assume a relaxed, open position that leaves space for conversation. If there is a very reserved and potentially dominated individual, I will physically turn my body toward them and ask them to contribute. That tells the dominant person that it's "not their turn" and opens the floor for someone else. And the final point is I smile a lot, even finding the right moment for humor.

Nothing dispels tension better than laughter.

Opening and Closing Acts

Sales Stages for Shorties

Put that coffee down. Coffee's for closers only.

—David Mamet

In this chapter you'll learn:

- The sales process as a three part story with a happy ending
- How to break the ice and not the china with customers
- Physical approaches to each part of a sales process
- Why being physical over the phone is attractive
- Not to overshadow prospective clients or your product

Many dramas have three acts: act one introduces the characters and sets the stage for the story; in act two the story unfolds, creating dramatic tension and intrigue; and then act three brings the story to its resolution. Within this structure there are comedies, where everything goes horribly wrong in the middle, but in the end everything comes right; there are tragedies, where the tensions throughout inevitably lead to bad, bad endings; and there are heroic adventures where the trials that appear destined to fail are fully overcome in the finale.

Like all of these dramatic cycles, many in sales would agree that their cycles are full of drama too. They transition from act to act and stage to stage, with each element of the journey playing out a predictable set of objectives to be achieved and obstacles to be overcome in order to get the desired ovation (the sale!) at the end of it all.

How you present yourself in each of these stages needs to align with those objectives to overcome the obstacle. Your *character* in all of this is the way you behave—the choices that you make in the situations of jeopardy presented to you. Your behavior under pressure determines the character (e.g., hero, villain, fool, victim, healer, virgin, to name but a few) that your customers, clients, and team can perceive you as. Choose to take your clients through the wrong drama and you may find the only character to play is the fool. But choose to take your customers through the right order of events, and you will always find moments to appear as the hero to them. So let's set the journey with some standard steps in the buying process for you to align your nonverbal behavior with and to avoid the traps and pitfalls of becoming the clowns and villains of the piece.

The Sales Stages

Zeami, the Japanese classical dramatic writer of the thirteenth century, wrote that stories have a traditional three-part narrative progression: Jo-ha-kyu, meaning anticipation-release-payoff. Tension builds, bursts into climax, and finishes quickly. All of this has similarities to the Western concept of Aristotle's three-part thesis, antithesis, synthesis. And so it is no different for the traditional sales "rule of three" form known as Introduction, Evaluation, and Close. Every company or product can have subcategories to these three principal stages of the sale, but to all intents and purposes these encompass the mechanics of any sales process. Let's look at each one close up:

1. **Introduction.** Like the first act of any play, its objective is to set the scene with the characters and context in anticipation of the conflicts that will unfold. For many organizations, the plot of this first act can include lead generation, where we introduce our company and offering to the buyer and try to make a connection that will trigger interest in evaluating our products or services against their needs. This act can also include our first meetings with the clients for the sale, during which the seller tries to identify the right allies for the buying side, and the buyer evaluates the sales team and begins to decide who is a friend, an enemy, or a dolt to be indifferent to.

    Completion of this act signals the buyer's and seller's readiness to move to the evaluation stage. If either the buyer or the seller is left unfulfilled with respect to either trust or credibility with each other, then there is very little point to moving to the next stage of the story—it will not be acted with any vigor or heart, and undoubtedly will fizzle out of energy for the third stage and die before it gets there.

2. **Evaluation.** Like any good story, this is where the most interesting action is released. Everyone gets busy looking at and focusing on the buyer's needs and comparing the options available to the customer's obstacles. As the story unwinds around the abilities of the seller's offerings to meet the buyer's needs, the end of this stage should see the buyer ready for some decisive action.

3. **Close.** Just as in the best plays, films, and books, the payoff leaves us in no doubt as to some of the most important elements of the rela-

tionship between the protagonists. This means the determining moment of "as much as a customer can shake hands and buy at the end of this story, he can shake hands and leave." Yes, bittersweet but nonetheless a decisive moment for all the parties. Unfortunately for badly executed sales cycles, this decision is often no decision at all, but an all too obvious outcome; but when there is a winner at this stage, it is in the stakes of how trust and credibility are paid off; and if not a sale this time, then there are still episodes or sequels in the franchise to play out over the long game.

So now that we know the basic plot, let's look at the ways to physically play each moment to maximize the levels of trust and credibility scored at each stage in order to improve your ratings and give you a competitive advantage. The verbal and nonverbal patterns and levels you are going to study here are all part of working toward Rapid Resonance™ between limbic brains.

Frankly, My Dear . . .

Take the example of a basic sale on a retail floor. Introductions in stores can follow a painfully consistent pattern—shopper enters the store and begins to browse the merchandise displays, and eventually a salesperson approaches and asks, "Can I help you?" They might insert a "Hello" in front of the question, but regardless, the answer from the shopper is virtually guaranteed to sound something like, "No thank you, just looking." The salesperson now walks away and "lurks," hoping the shopper will change her mind and ask for help.

There are a number of possible variations to this introduction. The clerk sometimes becomes immediately discouraged and so disappears altogether, impossible to find when the shopper *is* ready to be helped—and in these cases the shopper in return often mirrors that clerk's behavior and despondently exits the store and moves over to the competition. The key learning here is that the buyer and seller have not made a nonverbal or verbal "feeling" connection, and thus greeted and exited each other's company, their reptilian brains categorizing each other as "indifferent."

How can we change this introductory step, and how can we get from an indifferent category to a friend category? First, let us look at the initial greeting.

Toto, Did She Hurt You?

Generally, salespeople in these situations approach the shopper and position themselves close but in the visual periphery of that person's "social" space (remember our discussion on territory in Chapter 3, where this is a distance of 7 to 12 feet), or bolder still within the "personal" space. This can cause a natural suspicious "freeze" reaction in the buyer, ever so subtle, but it is there and you know you've felt it as a customer.

"Can I help?" the assistant then offers, usually winning the standard socially acceptable rebuttal, "Just looking," in order to see if the potential threat will withdraw out of the personal or social space and into a more public domain. If the assistant backs out of the buyer's "grazing territory," then they can relax and continue to peruse if the pastures of the store hold any great resource. But if the seller approaches too aggressively, invades the personal or intimate space, and even ignores the "just looking" response, then the shopper assumes "enemy," and this negative stereotype initiates a primal reaction: the shopper flushes and flees the store (either feigning some acceptable excuse, for example, looking at his watch or phone and retreating out into public safety, or backtracking and browsing his exit out).

Worse still, you might have even witnessed customers leap across a store with surprise because the assistant has blindsided them (moved fast into their peripheral vision within the personal distance—four feet away) due to their focus on the shiny merchandise. These customers often show a primal and very visible and vocal response of surprise, fear, and social embarrassment—not a great combination to start a sale!

Test this out yourself by observing customers in retail stores: notice the attitude they have as they enter the store, along with their rhythm of movement—for example, are they direct and quick or perhaps slow and tentative? Watch the eye contact they make with the merchandise in the store. What is your innate and instinctual theory as to how safe or risky their experience is right now? And what changes when an assistant comes into sight and starts to talk with them? Is there a marked change in their behavior? Does their muscle tone get softer or tenser? Do they get good eye contact or look away? Make a study of the interactions between customers and sales assistants in various stores and think about the ways body language and the behavior of the sales assistant could be changed in order to improve the experience and "safety" of the customer. Or if the assistant is looking to make great connections quickly, what is he doing physically that you think is facilitating this?

I Believe in America—America Has Made My Fortune

What if the salesperson did not approach the shopper? What if, instead, the salesperson assumed an inviting, nonthreatening TruthPlane posture and stood in plain sight well outside of the customer's social space when he appears? What might this feel like to a potential buyer?

Well, imagine that the sales assistant is already well in sight of the customer as he enters the store (yet not blocking the entry or taking up personal or social territory the customer may need to assess the goods). Imagine the shopper's reaction, seeing a salesperson standing there with an inviting come-talk-to-me posture? Maybe the salesperson doesn't do anything except smile when the shopper looks at her and subtly and quickly raises her eyebrows in the universal gesture of, "I recognize you." How will the shopper respond? It will be a friend response, or even a "potential sexual partner" response, depending on a number of other factors!

Now what if the salesperson then approaches the customer in clear view, front to him, calmly yet assertively so the customer views her as predictable and therefore nonthreatening (instead of approaching from behind and effectively "blindsiding" the customer—causing him to jump across the shop floor in surprise and fear and crash into the merchandise, as we've all seen on occasions)? The open body language, an "eyebrow flash" of recognition (read about this next), and a gentle smile—so as to say "All is good now"—while staying well outside of the customer's social, personal, or intimate territory—will inevitably draw the shopper to the salesperson, and the salesperson can now begin her communication within the social territory, with perhaps the polite, friendly greeting, "Hello, how are you today?"

This, by the way, is called by some in the field of psychology and communication a *phatic question*—one of the "customary" social niceties of casual interactions, not emotionally revealing and with a set social response: often, "Fine thanks. You?" We say these things not because we want to elicit a response, but rather because they smooth out any friction in our social interactions. They are at the low end of the vulnerability spectrum and thus polite territory to enter any conversation from the *perimeter* of the social space.

Rapid Recognition

The eyebrow flash or "rapid eyebrow raise" is universal (with some cultural modifications) as a sign of greeting, and is also used by some primates as a social greeting signal. Eyebrow movements in general play a major role in interpersonal communication in a variety of contexts. Surprise—positive and negative, flirting, approving, seeking confirmation, thanking, emphasizing, expressions of indignation, arrogance, asking questions; and in some cultures rejection, disapproval, and as a signal for "No." However, the eyebrow flash, specifically, is universally used as a way of expressing a "Yes" to social contact—either requesting it or approving a request.

Upon establishing visual contact, the head is usually lifted a bit and the eyebrows are then raised for approximately one-third of a second, while a smile simultaneously spreads: as a concluding gesture the person often nods. The eyebrow flash is generally used when some prior friendly relationship already exists and so will often not automatically appear when strangers are greeting each other. Therefore, we can see the power of performing this eyebrow flash gesture in sales situations where a feeling of familiarity is of benefit, and yet the two parties ordinarily are a long way off this in their relationship. Within this context, to express contact readiness and/or expressing some kind of assent or affirmation can bring huge advantage.

All We Want Are the Facts, Ma'am

One step deeper in but still in the Introduction, we get to a second level of vulnerability in any conversation, which is referred to by some as "factual" communication. This form of communication includes questions that elicit straightforward observations to which no strong opinions might be attached. You can see the benefit of this form of communication in that it can give you useful data that helps you move customers forward into Evaluation, that they are happy to give after some initial phatic communication; yet, they are most probably still not eliciting information or opinion that puts them at any physical or social risk. In the same way, you would not wish to be closer to them than their social space at this point. For the interaction in the store, this might sound like, "Is this your first time in our store?"

I Drink Your Milk Shake! I Drink It Up!

With the answers to factually based questions, you are ready to take the customer into revealing his views and opinions around the sales situation. This is a level up on a scale of vulnerability and further along the path of potentially moving the customer closer to "clicking," or connecting with you and revealing some evaluative data. The statements and questions you ask of the customer or client to elicit similar statements or questions in this same category are called "evaluative."

In the context of the store this could sound like: if the customer answered that he has not been there before to your above factual question, you can move him on to the evaluative question, "So, how do you like the way we've set out the store?" And if the customer has been to the store before, your evaluative question may sound like, "Welcome back, what did you like the last time you were here?" As you can understand, there is increased risk for both parties around the answers to these questions, that is, the evaluation of the customer could be negative: "I hate this store!" or "I've actually come back to complain!" In asking such questions and making such evaluative statements, we take a certain risk because we may take a position that is potentially in discord with others. Even so, the risk can often be limited, or even the chance of negativity quite low (if he's come back to the shop, it is hopefully because he wants to buy again!). The upside is that it elicits from the customer a movement toward expressing his values around the situation, and consequently moves you closer toward understanding his motivation for being in your environment today; that is, how he may evaluate the ability of the store to meet his needs, even though at this point you may not know exactly what piece of merchandise will fill that need.

The shopper and salesperson are now in the Evaluation phase of the sale, and the salesperson having achieved "friend" status with the shopper, can now take an active role in the evaluation and move into his personal space with a collaborative posture. Everything up to and including this point is essentially transactional—that is, communication that conveys *thought-oriented* as opposed to *emotionally oriented* information about the buyer. It's only when we cross the threshold to the emotional that we can have more connected interactions and be more willing to make ourselves vulnerable to others, thus opening up our personal space to them. Emotional information flow improves our chances of building a strong connection between the seller and buyer, which is of course a major advantage to the selling process.

Many retail sales never get beyond the transactional points. The average store clerk tends to think her role is to support the transaction process and tell the buyer about the product he is interested in, or worse, just play "Vanna doing a fetch and display" role to the buyer's selected items. However, many believe the salesperson has more to offer in support of the buyer and should seek to get involved in the shopper's decisions and help him consider his options thoroughly. And this begins by understanding what the shopper is looking for, why he is looking for it, and how he plans to use it. This calls for better questions and active listening, laid out in Chapter 5, to the responses.

It's Been Emotional

Let's consider that our example store sells sports shoes. One sales process might have the shopper bringing the salesperson a shoe from the rack and asking for a size nine, wide, and the salesperson dutifully running off to the basement to find a shoe that matches the request. A more engaged process would have the salesperson asking about the shopper's running habits, running style, past experience with shoes that worked well, identification of any issues around running, and many others. So now the salesperson is looking to make statements or ask questions that will elicit "emotional" statements or questions from the customer.

In this situation it might have the vocal quality of a questioning, upward intonation on the phrase, "How do you feel when you run?" Other non-verbal actions might have the salesperson look at how the customer walks or runs to identify pronation, supination, or any other foot stability issues. The retail salesperson could then describe for the shopper the types of shoes in the store that fit this profile, based on the abundance of experience she and her colleagues have built up from repeatedly asking these questions and observing the responses. All the while, the conversation has been conducted to reinforce the idea of this salesperson as "friend" and to drive up her trust and credibility quotient. With high scores, the salesperson has a good chance of hitting "trusted advisor" status to be able to make a shoe size, color, and style recommendation that will best suit the needs, lifestyle, and, most important, the desires and motivations of that shopper.

It is now time to grab some shoes and help the shopper try them on and validate the recommendations. Here is where the salesperson can enter the customer's intimate space with the opportunity to touch (within the appropriate limits of the shoe trade!). Gentle touch can increase levels of the hormone oxytocin—known for its effect on a part of the brain called the amygdala to reduce fear, anxiety, and stress and promote social bonding. Once again, questions that elicit emotions from the customer are of benefit. "How do they feel?" And this lays the territory and pathway to the highest level on the vulnerability scale, and so the most important statements or questions to ask in order to elicit and stand a chance of aligning with the customer's values. These are called peak or "self-reflective" questions or statements and elicit introspection. Remember that through all of these interactions it is critical that the salesperson maintain an engaged, supportive, and trustworthy stance during this "proof step" in the Evaluation stage.

I'll Have What She's Having!

Questions and statements that elicit introspection are essential for the proof stage of the sale, as they give data around the *values* and *beliefs* motivating the customer at this time. Self-reflective questions in the context of this shoe store might sound like, "How do these work with what is most important to you about running?" The answers that can be elicited from such a question are close to the apex of the vulnerability spectrum and increase your Rapid Resonance with the client; and so, if the salesperson comes no closer than the personal space (no intimate space close-talking) and keeps her body language open, affirming and accepting the statements that come back, the customer is inclined to view the sales professional as a friend of the tribe, that is, a *supplier* to the values and beliefs he holds as most important, and thus driving the customer's behavior toward the Close.

In all sales situations it is ideal to get the customer to agree to the hypothetical vision of buying the product or service before trying it out. The proof step should be one that confirms the recommended decision, rather than be the driver of which decision to make. In other words, too many salespeople—especially in retail, but not limited to that environment—depend too heavily on the product to sell itself. The reality is that the product will inspire shoppers to buy it only if they can *see* themselves using it. The goal of the salesperson, by actively listening to the triggers and motivation of the shopper, is to begin to enhance that vision of life with the product the shopper needs so as to make a closable buying decision. In the case of the sports shop, trying on the shoes is not about "Do I like it?" but "Is this shoe the one that will fulfill the objective of the purchase?" The objective could be a very emotional one, like, "Do I feel strong and fast in these?" If "Yes," then the Close has written itself.

Thank You, Sir. I'm Glad It's Off My Mind.

A retail Close, when backed up by a well-performed Introduction and Evaluation, becomes smooth and natural. If all your verbal and nonverbal communication has served to score high trust and credibility scores with the client, and a status as "friend," then the buyer will want to buy from *you*.

Now, you can begin to assume a far more assertive, leadership posture with the shopper. It will be subtle, but at this point it is appropriate to move yourself in front of the DoorPlane—make space again between the two of you and lead him to follow you to the point of sale. You can build a certain momentum on top of his inspiration to purchase. The customer is now clearly in a feeling of desire for the product or service, and needs to know the actions to take in order to Close. Simply help him by physically and verbally taking him through it. In retail, this can sound like, "Come on over to the checkout and let me wrap it up for you" as you move out of his space and make a direct route to the payment area of the store.

I Do Wish We Could Chat Longer

In contrast to the retail story, business-to-business (B2B) sales, though following the same basic structures, can quite often have some different dimensions. Physically the seller may travel to the client and often over long distances. And/or the seller can work more over the phone, or by other electronic communication methods. Mentally, the B2B buyer usually has some idea why she needs something and why she is talking to a salesperson, that is, the buyer should have no business reason to consciously browse. So the Introduction to a B2B sale can quite often begin on the telephone, where either the seller or the buyer has placed the call.

Maybe the buyer is responding to a lead generation effort from marketing, either directly or via the website. In any case, both buyer and seller in that first call are trying to decide if their relationship should begin to move forward now, or not. This is a difference from the retail sale, in that the B2B sale has an element of decision from both the seller and buyer regarding moving forward: in the first contact of the Introduction, both are qualifying the other. In order to find the right answer, it is essential to initiate an open dialogue, one based on trust. But does body language really matter when people are talking on the telephone?

For many people the response to this would be no, since how can body language be important if the caller can't see the person he's talking to? Well, of course as you've heard in earlier chapters, the primitive brain that evaluates us immediately as either friend, enemy, potential sexual partner, or as being indifferent to us, is looking out for nonverbal signals in order to make gut level judgments. And remember also, if the customer has insufficient nonverbal data to make a quick judgment, she will default to the most negative viewpoint, that is, you become the enemy. So it is in our interests to give maximum nonverbal data across the telephone. Now, of course you can see the compromise already—telephone has no visual content, which of course an audience is usually mainly relying on in order to make its judgment, so we need to enrich the nonverbal data in the tonality of the voice and also enrich the words we use, giving them more emotional content and painting more vivid pictures of our physicality and environment, and an emotional relationship to the customer or client on the other end of the line.

We have all heard the comment that you can *hear* someone smiling— and it is true. If we smile, our voice is lighter and higher and conveys happiness. If we show anger on our faces, the muscles affect our voice too—it will be deeper and more stressed. Facial expressions affect our voice, and our voice transfers key parts of a message to help the receiver understand what is being communicated. Whether the conversation takes place on the telephone or face-to-face, the facial expression, which is part of body language, plays a major role in the communication process.

The pace of the voice of people who are angry may be faster than normal, their voice may be deeper, their words may be clipped and sharp, and their breathing will no doubt be faster, which will also have an effect on how the words were uttered. Quite simply, their body language will have a massive effect on how the words are said, and that contributes to the nonverbal data in the sound of the message transferred, because when people speak on the telephone, their body language will still reflect their mood and feelings. It happens unconsciously.

Breathing patterns play a major role in how words are spoken. As the air from our lungs is exhaled, it passes over the vocal cords, which vibrate to make a sound. For the exhaled air to pass over the vocal cords smoothly, the passageway has to be clear. Crunch your body, and the passageway starts to become restricted. Restriction starts to happen when we sit down. This is because our normal reaction is to lower our head and shoulders. Try this simple exercise:

1. Stand tall and upright so the air passage is open and say, "Good morning."
2. Sit down and slump into your chair and say, "Good morning." Can you hear the difference?
3. Remain seated, but sit up in your chair, look ahead, and say "Good morning" again. Can you hear the difference this time?

Quite clearly, the position of the body has a fundamental effect on how words sound. When we are slumped, the words have a downward intonation, which could give someone listening to us the impression that we sound unhappy, unconcerned, or even bored and uninterested. This may not be the case—in fact it probably isn't—but that is the message the person we are talking to will receive. So, sitting with your hands and gravity in general in the GrotesquePlane when you are on a call—though perhaps more comfortable for you, as it takes less energy and maybe makes you feel personally more relaxed about the call—may have uncomfortable consequences for the client at the other end of the phone and therefore elicit a negative response. It will take more energy for you, but you will get better results if on the important sales calls over the phone you use the TruthPlane and the PassionPlane when you speak.

Because even a subtle physical impulse affects the vocal muscles to such a strong degree, when you use body language over the telephone, your audience can *hear* your intention more clearly; the key is to concentrate on physically projecting that intention rather than merely intending it psychologically.

Lead your audience members to become confident in you and in themselves by placing your hands and gestures open in the TruthPlane when you communicate with them, framing their access to your vulnerable belly area and bringing unconscious attention to it—even over the telephone—affects your voice in a profound way. And remember, when the arms hang down and the body is still, the voice follows and drops significantly in tone (another nonverbal indicator of the meaning behind a message). This deeper voice then tends to drop even further at the end of each thought, with a downward intonation that can easily signal sleep or depression if the voice is quiet, or aggression if the voice has volume.

The Dormant Sales Pro

If you wish to send a child to sleep with a story, just pitch the tone of your voice down at the end of each line of text, and start the next line at the deep tone you finished the last one on. So your voice drops down and down like a flight of stairs. The tone of voice informs the old brain that it is time to relax the body and decrease the breathing rate, heart rate, blood pressure, and brain activity.

Certain chemicals are sent around the body to tell the brain to start shutting down some of the nonvital functions, most importantly, the conscious mind. The child's skin begins to go paler and waxy in tone as her eyes glaze over and her limbs begin to go limp.

You see, it is not the story that sends us to sleep, but the tonality of the reading that gives us the instruction at a deep, deep level. And we have all certainly witnessed sales professionals who have put both themselves and their audiences to sleep in seconds with their downward-inflected tonality.

The Despondent Sales Pro

Next we look at the *depressed* downward tonality of the sales leader who tells us, "It's been a great year," but in a tone that says, "I am close to hanging myself . . . Dump any stock I've previously sold you, right now." As Dr. Mehrabian's studies concluded, given a choice between believing the content and believing the nonverbal messages, the unconscious mind will go with the nonverbal as being more trustworthy. Once again, hands down by the sides is a surefire route to creating a downturn in credibility.

The Despotic Sales Pro

Finally, there is the *loud-voiced* downward tonality, which is more prone to happen when the hands are down at the sides and the body is pacing or well in front of the DoorPlane. Pacing up and down in the space creates the overconfidence of being a moving target and puts more air into the lungs; the brain functions better with more oxygen intake and processes some of the fight-or-flight chemicals, so as not to depress and poison the system. However, the extra air volume in the lungs gives a loud, forceful downward inflection that can sound overtly commanding, especially when mixed with an adrenaline fueled attitude—a product of the aggressive "fight" response.

This may be acceptable to a customer who feels he is clearly under threat from somewhere else and can sense that dangerous uncertainty personally; such people will be attracted to a strong command structure in the tone of the voice. It will feel more certain and so safer. More often than not, however, in the modern sales world the commanding voice seems too aggressive and often just crazy. Trust disappears because the audience members cannot see for themselves the imminent threat to which the sales professional seems to be having a strong response.

The later stages of the Introduction and the second two stages of a B2B sale (Evaluation and Close) almost always involve multiple people in the selling and buying organization and can also often include more than one selling organization. They typically take multiple events, pass through many steps in each stage, and can require multiple rounds of decision making. From the perspective of nonverbal influence, the complex sale simply creates multiple circumstances where every lesson discussed so far in this book comes into focus.

Dealing with finding your winning body language among these complex situations is the work of the next chapter.

Chapter 6 Quick Study

Just as in any discipline, there are forms to follow, and sales has a simple pattern to it: the Introduction, Evaluation, and Close. Each of these steps in the sales process can occur within myriad places or times; however, the order is a principle, and breaking that order will undoubtedly break the relationship you are building. As the pattern moves forward, so too does the relationship, along with the way you can nonverbally relate in the space with a client or customer. The Introduction should be social, the Evaluation can be personal and even intimate, and the Close has an opportunity to be executed in the social space, bringing the journey full circle.

Just Do This Now

1. During the Introduction phase of a sale, keep your relationship within the social space, in order to keep the client or customer comfortable with your presence and allow him to get to know you and your product without any of pressures of personal intimacy.
2. In the Evaluation stage, know that there is an opportunity to lead the client into discoveries around how he values the service or product, in order for him to be fully motivated to buy. You can often move much closer to the client physically throughout this stage or move the meetings to more intimate, intense spaces.
3. Know that your body language counts over the phone too. Use everything you know about *Winning Body Language for Sales Professionals* when you are communicating electronically too.

Theory to Practice

There are products and services being sold using nonverbal stories all the time. Indeed it has been found in tests that information-laden logical ads don't excite the decision-making part of the brain as much as nonrational, more emotional image-laden ads.

Think about how you would sell if you did not have to deliver any facts and could simply show action and emotion to your buyers in order to compel them through your behavior rather than convince them through your intellect. What would your pitch be like if you could bypass the rational analysis and appeal directly to your customer's emotions?

Now that you've imagined this, how much of it might you credibly be able to add to your normal pitches, presentations, or selling style in order to speak to their real decision brain?

A Body of Knowledge

Farrell Macdonald (farrellmacdonald.com) is a top producing Realtor with Coldwell Banker Terrequity Realty in Toronto. He is a master at helping clients make fully informed decisions by educating them—rather than selling to them. A warm personality and a witty presenter, he is loved by everyone who meets him. Here he talks about how he physically works a space with sellers to bring them the buyers they need.

Tall Orders

When I list a property for sale, I first need a tour of the home. The space is foreign to me, but very familiar to the sellers. Although my personal opinion is irrelevant, I still need to make observations and suggestions from a *buyer's perspective.* In other words, I am charged with a professional mandate in a very personal space.

The seller needs to be unthreatened by me. But since I stand six and a half feet tall, any conversation that follows the tour is best had sitting down! Not only is this more comfortable for us all, but it allows me to sense a seller's unspoken signals.

For example: restlessness or rigidity may signal reluctance or resistance to ideas for improvement from a buyer's viewpoint.

Sitting together also allows me to maintain appropriate eye contact—critical in any culture to establishing trust. And more important, this setting allows me to send some of my own unspoken signals. As Mark Bowden has taught: gesturing from the midriff (the TruthPlane)—revealing my vulnerability—allows my prospective clients to feel at ease and to trust that what I am telling them is true. Most important, it also ensures that I remain to be seen calm and assertive. And even more important—a respectful guest in their home.

In real estate, the path from foreign to the familiar can be traveled without uttering a single word.

Michael Leckie (michael@leckie.org) works for the world's leading technology advisory services and research company. He is a business leader and quite a brilliant manager, responsible also for his group's talent development efforts globally. His personal mission is to make the world a better place to work and live—one organization at a time. Here he talks about how he purposefully constructs his environment to connect nonverbally with his prospects—even over long distances.

Physical Phone FX

Winning Body Language is something that I use most often when no one can see me. Working with people all over the globe, face-to-face meetings can sometimes be impossible. And yet it is often a conversation with me that can trigger a potential customer to buy, or not. So naturally I need to connect immediately—and over the phone.

I make sure I have the environment I'm calling from exactly how I would want it if the prospective client were with me in person—free of all distractions. Then I communicate in a way that is comfortable yet energized and always fully present. For me this is standing and using the TruthPlane. I am a former consultant, and I spent a lot of time at whiteboards. So I still do this when on the phone. I'll draw up simple diagrams and take the prospective client through the process step-by-step saying, "Picture this . . . now imagine what I'm drawing right now . . . you can see it in your mind right?" Then I will keep referring back to the picture, walking them quickly through what is relevant and useful. Finally I can take a quick photo of it with my iPhone and send it in an e-mail as a reminder of our conversation. All these things remind me that I am focused on connecting with the prospective client and being awake, engaged, and happy to be right there with that person at that time . . . even when I am not physically there at all!

Niki Winterson (nikiwinterson.com) was an actress and producer before becoming a top-performing sales presenter on the QVC shopping TV channel. She went on to head Theatre, Film, and Television at Global Artists agency in London and is now one of the United Kingdom's top talent agents as CEO of Wintersons. Here she talks about how she used her nonverbal communication to create a character to gain access to hearts and minds at home—selling to millions.

Physical Relations in the Home

Body language is an essential part of selling on TV. The audience's initial introduction to you is entirely visual, and it is therefore vital that they understand the message your body is communicating. A great deal of thought has to be given to how one can best use body language to sell a product, and luckily I have worked with Mark Bowden, who is a careful and thoughtful guide; also, when I worked as a top sales presenter, broadcasting across Europe's shopping television, I personally spent a long time working out the best way of presenting both myself and each product I sold, in visual terms. As

I developed my ideas, I began to study the performances of the other demonstrators and noticed that the most successful ones took great care of three special relationships:

1. Their relationship with the customer
2. Relationship with the camera
3. And most important, their relationship with the product

With your TV *relationship with the customers,* put simply, you're a virtual guest in their home. We know when we enter someone else's space that there are rules, and that we should show what we might call good physical manners. We do not occupy the space selfishly, for instance.

My manner on television was always that of someone who would respect your space, your home, and your possessions. In the first 20 seconds of any demonstration of the product, I would use small, contained, movements—not constrained, for it was important that I looked natural, but contained—so that mentally I didn't look like the sort of person who would knock over your ornaments! I always sold "in character"—my technique was to create a persona which was basically the same as the customer—I was a hardworking housewife who used these products because they helped me run a busy life within a loving family. I would be sure to mention my husband and kids a lot in the demonstrations, because I knew from talking to Mark that when we mention something we really love, our body will communicate the truth of that feeling—and that was important to me, to establish myself as a person with "true" relationships, because if the audience were convinced of my sincerity as a person, they would be convinced of my genuine respect for the product too.

With the *relationship to the camera,* it is very important to think of the demonstration as a drama in which the product was the star or "hero," and I was, in physical terms, the "sidekick" or guest star. It was a very important rule never to place anything between the product and the camera. Never lean over the product or place myself between the product and the live camera.

The third and most important use of body language is in the *relationship with the product* itself. The number one rule: *always handle the product with respect.*

I have seen funny, talented presenters who tried to be "pals" with the product and play equal status to it. This can make for fun television but generally sees sales fall. Put simply, the product has to be more important than the sales presenter.

To this end, a great technique I used was to make it a mantra that in physical terms, the product solves my problems. So, for instance, when talking about a labor saving product, I would always give the product what I thought of as "talismanic power": when talking about the product, I would refer to it with a tiny nonverbal hint of reverence—head slightly inclined, hands together in front of me, not in prayer but in deference. And when I touched it, a weight would fall from my shoulders. I'd stand straighter, taller.

Always think of yourself as a person whose problem—physical, emotional, domestic, whatever—could be cured by the product. If you think that mentally, your body language will communicate it in the subtlest but most powerful ways.

The Complex Sale

Campfire Signing

*There is never any justification for things being complex
when they could be simple.*

—Edward de Bono

In this chapter you'll learn:

- Whom to seat where at complex sales events
- To manage the environment to support the right meeting culture
- Simple strategies for building community around change
- Powerful positioning for introductions, presentations, and closings
- How a great comic leads the community to listen

A "complex sale" describes a sale in which the seller must meet the needs of multiple influences on a buying decision. This type of sale is most often but not exclusively found inside of business-to-business (B2B) sales environments, because one of the common attributes of a complex sale is that there are multiple people on both the buying and selling side. Either way, in a complex sale the buyer's requirements are inherently complex, with multiple dimensions to be addressed.

Often, the buying decision will be mission critical, at least at the departmental level if not the strategic level, and so could involve significant change for the buyers. For many of the people on the buying side, the decision will influence their position in the company, perhaps even their careers. For the sellers, typically, each successful complex sale is a milestone in reaching their annual sales goal. In other words, the stakes are typically high for everyone. No pressure, then!

All Together Now

The complexities of these types of sales generally lead to long sales cycles full of meetings and conversations; these sales can last weeks, months, even years before closing. For some very large strategic complex sales, the account development will stretch across multiple complex sales cycles and closing events. In other words, if you do complex sales, you are a sales professional involved in these accounts for an extended period of time and so will need to get along with everyone while you try to achieve your goals—and they are going to need to get along with you!

In addition to taking a long time, these multilevel sales, complete as they are with the meeting of and working with lots of other people, mean that you need to work *within the tribe of the customer* to achieve your goals. The latter part is interesting because you are trying to be accepted into this tribe, at least temporarily. Consider for a moment that the goal of all solution sellers in complex sales situations is to achieve the status of *trusted advisor.* This requires that you fit into the social hierarchy of the customer's tribe. This credibility is earned through your insights, how you treat people, and the borrowed credibility that comes from whom you know in the organization, along with how the senior status individuals lend you their status as the process moves forward.

Ideally, trusted advisors have a status that inserts them into the social groupings at a level that helps them lead and facilitate the customer in making a decision to buy. The deeper you can create feelings of familiarity for yourself within these groups, the more likely it is that you will be seen as part of the tribe. Imagine the potential influence on your sales goals if you had a matrix of contacts within your customer's tribe who saw you as part of the team working toward *their* objectives. From this integrated status, many different opportunities arise to influence the outcome of the sale. The value to a salesperson of being such an advisor is that you can work inside and outside of a tribe at the same time, which creates a fascinating perspective with multiple points of leverage to help move the sale forward.

In this chapter we will discuss how, through a greater awareness of the environments in which the many critical communication events happen in these long complex sales, a salesperson can increase the likelihood of being accepted within the customer's complex organization and achieve the special status of trusted advisor needed to close successfully. Aligning your body language to fit within the complex groupings should become a key component of your overall sales strategy. It will allow you to evolve from a passive new entrant into a leader within the customer's hierarchical organization—guiding stakeholders to the right answers.

Supporting Your Sales Events Physically

The complex sale typically involves multiple people from both the buying and selling organizations, especially in the evaluation and selection phases. In Chapter 5 we discussed some simple physical circumstances and how they affect relationships, and now we will build on those lessons within the complex sale context. As the seller, particularly the lead salesperson in a complex sales cycle event, you always focus on creating the right group environment to support your call objective, and on managing the space to ensure you have optimized the situation to support nonverbal communication that will help bring the attendees together with aligned collaborative intentions.

So when planning a sales event, it is essential to know your objectives. As obvious as this sounds, many salespeople do not give this step the care and attention it deserves. The clearer you are about your sales objectives in that call, the easier it is to create an effective plan. Also, the more you understand the buyer's objectives in the call, the easier it is to achieve those objectives, which typically in turn support your objectives.

In addition to the "published" meeting objectives, there is also a private set of objectives for the salesperson. These relate to: you understanding what kind of support you are gaining, testing to see if you are making progress, evaluating relationships, understanding the tribe, and setting up the sale for success. These objectives are often achieved by seeing how people work with you, with each other, the questions that are asked, the questions that are answered, and how everyone acts toward one another. The environment can have a significant impact on the achievability of these objectives: in managing the physical spaces to allow you to leverage your awareness of how nonverbal communication can influence and persuade, you gain greater opportunities to put one more paddle in the water, giving more momentum to the certainty of closing the sale in your favor.

Spaces: Environments and Culture

The goal is to create a situation where the environment naturally invites people to feel connected and to avoid letting people fall into distributed positioning patterns that promote separateness or even confrontation. It is a dance, and the most important thing to remember as the sales choreographer is that you cannot let people know you are organizing the dance: who attends, the music, and the dance cards. The goal of the sales choreographer is to get all the dancers on the floor in the best place without their knowing they have been placed on purpose: it should all feel natural, as if the positioning is what any close group of collaborators would take with each other.

Before jumping into the specific examples, here are two spatial concepts for reference. The first concept is the idea of *triads,* and this of course leans heavily on work done alongside John King and Dave Logan, the writers of *Tribal Leadership*. They discuss the power of people working together in groups of three, a triad. The basic idea is that in a triad each individual is responsible for supporting the relationship of the other two. In other words, an individual's role is to work on helping the other two connect, communicate, get the most out of his or her interaction, and stay that way. Logan and King use this basic working structure as the fundamental unit to build a matrixed interconnected tribal organization that can work together, collaborate, and achieve great things.

This is a powerful perspective that helps the seller understand and accept responsibility for getting everyone to work together. The more you can set up physical spaces to promote a sense of triads among the people in a room, the easier it is to invoke the natural habits of the social (limbic) brain to draw people together. (We will look at how to build and integrate the triad formation shortly in the "Meeting Cultures" section.)

The second concept we would like to introduce is the metaphor of the "campfire." When you think of a campfire, you probably think of a friendly, even familiar place. For most of us a campfire is a place we gather with only direct family or familiar tribes. It also calls for the idea of a central focus—the fire—around which the participants direct their attention. Some may even be assigned different duties related to the fire, from collecting wood, adding wood, and roasting marshmallows to singing a song or two for everyone to join in on the chorus.

Meanwhile, traditional business meetings and seating arrangements promote numerous opportunities to let people fall into antagonistic—or at least certainly less communal—position patterns. As a salesperson trying to enter a tribe and promote collaboration, these less communal position patterns are often counterproductive. The goal is to get everyone around the campfire and to bring the triads into place to ensure that everyone feels naturally pulled to work together.

The success of group meetings is affected by the size, furnishings, and environmental conditions of the meeting space. The furniture arrangement within a meeting space also affects the nature of interaction and participation among group members, which in turn determines the social influence of certain members of the group and ultimately how decisions are made. Seating arrangements are usually left up to chance, but where meeting participants sit can influence overall meeting effectiveness. There are some classic structures of the way you can arrange seating at a meeting. Just like the other behaviors, nonverbal communication and body language that we look at in this book, those structures create environments that promote specific outcomes negatively or positively toward the sale.

In many cases, as a salesperson, you do not have control of your meeting environment, but in some cases you do, and here are some ways you can positively influence your meeting outcome through environment by choosing a seating arrangement suitable to your meeting type. Prior to your meeting, consider the number of people and the level of interaction and meeting goals. Then match the seating arrangements accordingly based on the following cultural criteria.

Meeting Cultures

During the complex sale, people are going to come together and communicate throughout the sales stages and with objectives that relate to the demands of that stage. To support these different events, the salesperson will find himself inside one of three basic meeting cultures: Collaboration, Presentation, and Decision.

We call them "cultures" because the different meetings have different behaviors, rules, and customs that are naturally invoked. This is then complicated by the space the meeting is held in and the natural environment that space creates. It will be an environment that supports the culture or conflicts with it; for example, ever tried to use the corner of someone's desk to create an interactive presentation when it is covered in reports and empty coffee cups? As stated earlier, unfortunately the salesperson often cannot control the space of the meeting, but regardless of that space, the salesperson still needs to attain the appropriate meeting culture to improve the chances of achieving the meeting objectives.

Let's examine the meeting cultures:

1. **Collaboration.** When salespeople are working with the buyer to qualify an opportunity, activate a trigger, do discovery, or plan a buying process event, they are in this mode. Collaboration simply means an interactive process with people who are essentially equals working toward a common goal: let's build this fire together. This meeting culture requires a high level of interaction, so the physical arrangements of seating must reflect *equality*. Equal contribution of ideas is easier when people are seated in a *circular* pattern: the campfire! Avoid positioning people in obvious positions of power, and instead seek round table arrangements that foster a feeling of contribution, collaboration, and community for all meeting participants (Figure 7.1).

2. **Presentation.** When salespeople are "presenting" to or facilitating an audience of buyers, either doing product demonstrations, PowerPoint, proposals, or making business cases, they are in the mode of facilitator with audience (Figure 7.2.). As sellers, this puts you and your team in front of your audience. The goal, in alignment with gaining collaboration and connecting with the tribe, is to have these meetings as

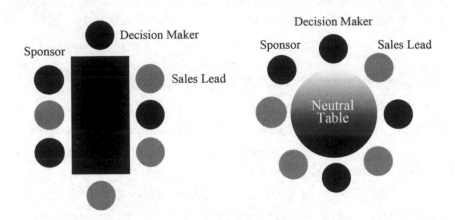

Figure 7.1   Collaborative Meeting Seating

interactive as possible. Presenters and facilitators need to move freely throughout the group, work one-on-one with individuals, and through hand gestures connect different "questioners" and "answerers" into dynamic triads, as introduced earlier in this chapter.

For example, when a buyer representative asks a question that the sales facilitator needs a supporting sales engineer to answer, the sales facilitator should position himself to form the top of a triangle: keeping his hands in the TruthPlane, stretching his arms out to form the lines of the triangle to connect the other two. Maintain this comfortable positioning throughout the dialogue, help them to connect and understand each other, and make sure the questioner is answered. The facilitator will be constantly creating these triads through the course of the presentation. Imagine the facilitator as a spotlight, constantly moving to bring different group members to center stage and make them look and feel good.

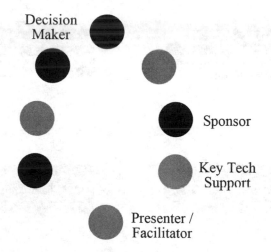

Figure 7.2   Presentation Positioning

3. **Decision.** Meetings at which decisions have to be made are complex dances because the power in the room must always appear to be in the hands of the decision maker, but the salesperson, potentially with the cooperation of a buyer power sponsor, must lead the meeting to the decision outcome. It is a meeting where the seller may move in an instant from being passive, flexible, and receptive to assertive, firm, and projecting; and then maybe back again. It is an environment where all of the status earned toward *trusted advisor* must be used carefully. The buying decision maker must walk away from this meeting feeling confident and fulfilled, but at the same time the salesperson must get what he wants: a close.

Meeting at the Boardroom

In business environments the most common space for complex sales events is the boardroom or meeting room in the buyer's or seller's office.

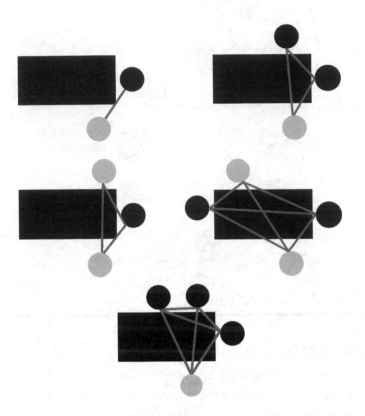

Figure 7.3   Triad and Campfire Settings

The boardroom table is an interesting environment that poses some interesting challenges. The shape of a boardroom table is typically rectangular, with single chairs at the head and foot and the same number of chairs along each facing side. This geometry has proven psychological impacts on how people interact. The control or power seats are at the head and foot of the table. People in these seats feel in control of the meeting, even if it is not their meeting. Side-facing seats are more peer-oriented.

Getting the geometry right to support a collaborative nonconfrontational environment becomes more complex with the more people you put in the room. Let us look at some combinations (Figure 7.3):

- **One-on-One.** Sit across if possible at a 90 degree angle to each other, although consider setting it up for the buyer to sit at the head or foot of the table. The reason we like this latter arrangement is that, although it suggests a power arrangement in favor of the buyer, it actually creates a body language opportunity to pull away from the table and offer a full torso view, but with security for the buyer at the corner of the table. The table and the buyer's position create comfort and a sense of safety; then, as you the seller pull back from the table, while sitting, you give the buyer the full inviting TruthPlane view of you. The table then is an anchor for the buyer, but not a barrier to you. Also, if you end up presenting anything, the corner of the table forms a natural point of a triangle to kick in triadic collaboration.
- **Two Buyers and One Seller.** Watch for a potential power play as to which one of the buyers may go for the head of the table. With the two buyers positioning themselves at a 90-degree angle to each other, on one corner side of the table, with yourself forming the third corner of a triangle, you have an instant triad to manage. Push yourself back just a little from your edge of the table and get in the habit of facing each person as he or she speaks. If the two of them are talking to each other, then you can engage in supporting their dialogue.

  Another way to leverage this situation, however, is for you as the seller to take the head of the table if you want to position yourself as higher in the social ranking than the people you are meeting with, that is, because it is an early meeting with the goal to get to a higher authority in the buyers' company, or after coming from higher authority with a firm mandate (and it can even be a way of implying a firm mandate exists when it does not). But of course this is ultimately risky, with its high potential to cause discomfort for the buyers.

- **Two Sellers and One Buyer.** It is strongly recommended to invite the buyer to sit at the head of the table and have you and your sales partner sit on either side. The heightening of the buyer's status by positioning her at the "head" countermeasures any anxiety around being outnumbered.
- **Two and Two.** The natural tendency is to take the adversarial model and line up two across the table. Though this can work out okay, it is worth experimenting with pairings, buyer and seller on each side. This inspires a more collaborative approach. The feeling is a shift of focus to the speaker; so two sellers focus on a speaking buyer or two buyers on a speaking seller. The fourth person is in a comfortable position to observe and facilitate. Think of it as overlapping triads.
- **One Seller and Three Buyers.** Push to have at least one buyer in an end seat. One, this should indicate the power in the team. Two, it encourages more of a campfire model. Now the seller is just one more person around the campfire and can focus on all three buyers equally.

Work toward your preferred seating arrangement. It forces a change from the traditional "us versus you" boardroom sales environment. Your goal is to break down the power play and create a campfire model. These actions do not have to be overt; rather, they need to be subtle changes that allow all participants to see as much of each other as possible, which usually means minimizing the use of the table for defense. The table can be used for safety, but not defense. If you can get the triads flowing, rather than gang versus gang, and build a campfire environment that warms everyone up, you will inspire the meeting toward an aligned conclusion. The geometry will support the instinct for community and collaboration.

Power, Place, and Stanford

When it comes to examining the power behind exactly how you set up an environment in order to influence and persuade the outcomes, an extreme example is the Stanford Prison Experiment.

In 1971, psychologist Philip Zimbardo, former classmate of Stanley Milgram (who is best known for his famously shocking obedience experiment), was interested in expanding upon Milgram's research. He wanted to further investigate the impact of situational variables on human behavior, so he set up a mock prison in the basement of Stanford University's psychology building and then selected 24 undergraduate students to play the roles of both prisoners and guards.

The simulated prison included three six-by-nine-foot prison cells. Each cell held three prisoners and included three cots. Other rooms across from the cells were utilized for the prison guards and warden. One very small space was designated as the solitary confinement room, and yet another small room served as the prison yard. The 24 volunteers were then randomly assigned to either the prisoner group or the guard group. Prisoners were to remain in the mock prison 24 hours a day for the duration of the study. Guards, on the other hand, were assigned to work in three-person teams for eight-hour shifts.

After each shift, guards were allowed to return to their homes until their next shift. Researchers were able to observe the behavior of the prisoners and guards using hidden cameras and microphones.

While the Stanford Prison Experiment was originally slated to last 14 days, it had to be stopped after just 6 days due to what was happening to the student participants. The guards became abusive, and the prisoners began to show signs of extreme stress and anxiety. While the prisoners and guards were allowed to interact in any way they wanted, the interactions were generally hostile or even dehumanizing. The guards began to behave in ways that were aggressive and abusive toward the prisoners, while the prisoners became passive and depressed. Five of the prisoners began to experience such severe negative emotions, including crying and acute anxiety, that they had to be released from the study early. Even the researchers themselves began to lose sight of the reality of the situation. Zimbardo, who acted as the prison warden, overlooked the abusive behavior of the prison guards until graduate student Christina Maslach voiced objections to the conditions in the simulated prison and the morality of continuing the experiment.

According to Zimbardo and his colleagues, the Stanford Prison Experiment demonstrates the powerful role that the situation can play in human behavior. Because the guards were placed in a position of power, they began to behave in ways they would not normally act in their everyday lives or in other situations. The prisoners, placed in a situation where they had no real control, became passive and depressed.

Theater Style

Typically, meetings with multiple participants on both buying and selling sides fall into the Presentation meeting culture, and often in "theater style" meetings. In the proof phases, and even the closing phases of a sales process, the theater style room provides a powerful setting. These rooms are designed, generally, to support the culture of presentation and interactive facilitation. In many B2B complex sales there will be demonstrations and presentations by the vendors. As sellers, this puts you and your team in front of your audience. If these meetings can be done inside of theater style rooms, it is a great advantage, as these rooms are designed to support interaction. Using the TruthPlane effectively in these spaces can help bond the facilitator and presenters to the audience.

Generally there are three types of Presentation (theater) configurations: boardroom, classroom, and U-shaped. In a business environment, U-shaped is preferred since it allows the facilitator and presenter to move within the audience area.

- The U-shaped arrangement promotes equality and participation. But if a Presentation meeting must use a boardroom, then try to turn the boardroom into a theater. The buyers should occupy the head of the table, and the sellers the bottom. The presentation materials, screen, etc., should be at the presenter's end of the room. From this spot the presenter/facilitator can move and use gestures to promote triads and a campfire affect. For example, when a buyer representative asks a question that the sales facilitator needs a supporting sales engineer to answer, the facilitator should position herself to form the top of a triangle: keeping her hands in the TruthPlane, stretching the arms out to form the lines of a triangle to connect the other two. Maintaining this comfortable positioning throughout their dialogue helps them to connect and understand each other and makes sure the questioner is answered. The facilitator will be constantly creating these triads through the course of the presentation.
- Classroom styles are risky, as they create an "us and them" setup that separates the facilitators and presenters from the audience. This is especially true if the classroom style has tables or desks in

front of each row of seating. In these situations, place the visuals at the front of the room, and try if possible to keep a pathway open along either side of the seating. This can allow a facilitator to move up and down along the sides in support of a prime presenter at the front. It will create larger triads than the intimacy of the U-shaped theater but is one way to break down the "us and them" environment to support interaction.

The Office Meeting

The desk is the most obvious power symbol in any communication situation. In a buyer's office, you are in the bear's den; if the buyer is the executive, he's a bigger bear. In this space the buyer feels in control and powerful. However, this can work in your favor (as the seller), as your buyer will likely feel comfortable, and as long as you work within the room's context, he can actually be very approachable. This environment creates many interesting opportunities for body language:

- **Executive Office.** This is first denoted by its size. Next it might even be clean, as this is a thinking person's desk. Finally, you might get lucky and be in with a real executive with a small meeting table with a couple of chairs. If this is the case, you are actually in a small meeting room not an executive office. These offices are sometimes used for qualifying, activating triggers, doing discovery, presenting business cases, and closing sales.

    Part of this space is a personal office and part of it is a close social meeting space. And if it has large internal windows and the blinds are open, it is now a public space! Be aware if you are invited for a private one-on-one, social meeting, or public performance. You also need to be adaptable for the proxemics and tribal nature of the meeting changing on a dime from a quick "get to know you" into a full-on public meeting. Always be prepared to move to a new stage in the sales cycle, relationship, or communication style to fit with the circumstance. In short: stay adaptable.

- **Contact's Office.** The challenge with this office setting is usually its size. Unlike an executive office, these spaces are usually very utilitarian. Yes, they have chairs, but they are probably simple affairs, neither comfortable nor flexible. Typically between the seller and buyer there is a desk full of clutter. In other words this office is not designed for entertaining; it is designed for work. Sellers find themselves in these offices usually early in a sales cycle for qualifying and maybe even discovery.

  A classic sign that a buyer is in the Choices phase of the buying process is a meeting that begins in one of these cramped spaces. You are entering the buyer's work space because this search is a worker task now, not a strategic endeavor. This can be a difficult environment for a salesperson to feel comfortable in, as it screams to the seller, "You are wasting your time and not dealing with power!" The buyer is likely to be very comfortable, since he sits in that chair all day, every day. At this point in the sales process, where you find yourself in this type of office, keep in mind you want to connect to the buyer. Make sure you sit back from the desk, keep your posture strong and alert, and keep yourself in the TruthPlane.

Do not let the desk become a barrier or a shield. You are always working to create accord and take away discord. And although this may be contrary to some selling styles or sales strategies that recommend putting fear into the buyer, this is not the strategy here.

Fear Is Dumb

The methods of "selling to the reptilian brain" may not be as useful as you might imagine within a complex B2B sales situation. It is true that many decisions are based on fear, and the primitive, reptilian brain is particularly attuned to detecting fear. Yet in the case of a complex sale, instead of promoting fear, you should use your nonverbal communication to calm the reptilian brain, which affords you a greater opportunity for your ideas to make there way through to the buyer's neocortex where complex ideas are able to be processed.

Chapter 7 Quick Study

A complex sale will often be "mission critical" to a business and could involve significant change for the multiple people on the buyer's side. The decisions made could influence their position in the company, as well as their careers. For the seller, the sale could be a milestone too. Work toward your preferred seating arrangement. There are typically high stakes and high stress for everyone; therefore, your goal in meetings is to break down the power play enough to create a campfire model where the traditional "us versus you" boardroom sales environment is reduced, and the geometry of the meeting will support the instinct for community and collaboration needed to push a sale as big as this forward.

Do This Now

1. Work toward meetings with three or more in the room to create more community and stability around the ideas.
2. Create seating arrangements that push competing "gangs" into one community with an equal status among the members.
3. At decision points, mark out the decision maker with a high status position.

Theory to Practice

Before any important meeting, it is always worth spending a few minutes thinking carefully about the seating arrangements. The key to success is intelligence (getting all the data together and thinking about it); preparation (thinking and acting through how you wish the meeting to perform); and adaptability (being able to change as the environment around you changes). Here's one way to do all of this:

> **Intelligence.** Get blank postcards and write the name of each participant (including yourself) on a card along with any important data about the participant that is pertinent to the meeting.
>
> **Preparation.** Place the cards in formation as you think the seating should best be for the meeting to move forward the way you need it to.
>
> **Adaptability.** Get a colleague in to look at the arrangement and to question you on the people, relationships, and rationale for the positioning at the meeting. Have the mindset to change things based on what you learn from your colleague's questions about the setup, and be ready to change things at the meeting too, for whatever reason.

Now, the only question left is how do you get everyone into these positions? Come early to the meeting with any materials needed for the meeting with the participants' names on the front cover. Lay them out in the arrangement required, and they are very likely to take the seats prescribed.

A Body of Knowledge

Jack Milner (standupanddeliver.co.uk) runs one of the United Kingdom's most innovative training companies and uses his background in comedy to help businesspeople move the stuff that gets in the way of communicating at their best. We all know a little laughter can help seal the deal, and as Jack has said many times, "When they're laughing—they're listening!" and leading others to laugh can be a welcome relief from the leader in any long sales cycle. Here he talks about the three nonverbal ways a comedian wins the trust and attention of an audience and how this can relate to sales.

Comedy Body Language Wins Them Over

Just as a good salesperson takes charge of the "conversation," so a good comic has to boss his audience and let them know he's in charge. As soon as a comedian walks on stage, the audience decides on his suitability as "leader." This is also true of the salesperson.

There's a certain quality top comics have as they walk on that makes the audience lean forward in anticipation. You just know they're going to be good. Conversely, and terrifyingly for any novices, the audience also knows if the comic hasn't got what it takes. The buzz evaporates, there is a cold silence in the room, and as the comic opens his mouth, his words hang unwanted in the air before disappearing into an echoey void. And from that moment on, it's going to be extraordinarily hard to win back the audience. This can be just as true in the sales conversation. Start off giving the wrong impression and there's no way back.

So what is the good comic "doing" that is different?

I believe three things are happening here.

The first is the desire to tell his story. The good comic wants to be in the space. So in body language terms he is looking at the audience, walking forward toward the action.

The second is the building of instant rapport. The body language and face are "open." Mark Bowden is much better than me on the specifics—but the comedian is, through open body language, building a connection with his audience.

Third, his walk reveals the style and personality of the comedian. We instantly "get" the comic persona through the rhythm he has when walking on stage. And the authenticity of this is vital to the comedian's success.

The desire to tell a story, to be open and communicate a persona to the audience, means we trust the comedian the moment he walks onstage. And in the end we are much more likely to buy from the person we like and trust than the unlikable and untrustworthy person, however good the product.

Tamara Glick is the founder of Trademark Image Consulting (trademarkimage.ca) and has been working with individuals and corporate clients to develop their distinctive, authentic style for over 15 years. She combines her background in communication, fashion, and image with her corporate experience in advertising and marketing, and this expertise is sought after by the media nationwide. Here she talks about how to fit in at the top table with any tribe as a female sales professional.

Image Savvy Tips for Female Sales Executives

For as many options as there are for women's business dress, there are just as many pitfalls. The trick to finding the right balance of personality and professionalism lies in the ability to read the silent language of your clients' corporate cultures. Accurately reflecting this in your work wardrobe can simultaneously meet your clients' expectations and cause you to stand out from the crowd in the right way.

The Culture You're Working Within

- A sea of dark suits indicates a corporate environment. So, depending on whether skirts or pants are your preference, it's time to invest in fine quality items that follow . . . suit.
- If women only wear skirt suits to work, you've found a traditional, formal corporate workplace. Pants are not unacceptable here, but look forward to knee-length skirts in flattering, business-appropriate styles (pencil, A-line, or fluted) with tailored jackets.
- Colorful, casual office? Inject personality into your outfits, and use creativity to set yourself apart. Up the ante with coordinated outfits in interesting colors, patterns, or fabrics.

Getting Dressed

- Find the "sweet spot": this is the intersection of the Audience (to whom you're selling) + Your Industry (what you sell) + Your Position (greater seniority = greater liberties).
- What qualities would be most relatable to in your position? Universally appreciated are polish, consistency, and professionalism. Begin here when building your work wardrobe.
- What's your Style DNA? Adding a personal touch to your work wardrobe creates individuality, generates appropriate conversation, and can make you memorable among peers.

Winning Wardrobe

- **Nimble Neutrals.** Ensure consistency in your wardrobe by building around two classic neutrals that are great on you.
- **Mix 'n' Match.** Choose a series of well-tailored pieces that create variety with a sense of cohesion.
- **First-Class Fit.** Reserve a portion of your wardrobe budget for professional tailoring to ensure an ideal fit.

Keep clothing freshly laundered and pressed. Check for wear on a regular basis, and be known for your attention to detail!

C-Suite Selling

Sight Beyond Sight

*Treating illnesses is why we became doctors. Treating patients
is what makes most doctors miserable.*

—Dr. Gregory House

In this chapter you will learn:

- The new role of Complex Sales Professional
- How to walk through like a "Challenger"
- Provocative models for executive business-based sales
- Executive Presence: standout C-suite behavior
- When to ask and when to listen in sales

The Internet is changing the role of salespeople in the buying process. It is time to think seriously about what these changes are going to mean for all salespeople. This chapter will help you deal with how the Internet is changing the role of the B2B salesperson in the complex sale using your nonverbal communication.

Back in the old days—and they are not that far back, say the 1990s—salespeople had a lot more control within the buying process, particularly around information. The statistics say salespeople used less than 10 percent of the materials produced by marketing in their sales cycles. The reason for this is that in the complex sale, the salesperson was often shaping the company's position and value into a context relevant to the prospect. In other words, the salesperson often had control of the message. What the customer understood about the selling organization came primarily from the salesperson, and often face-to-face. Salespeople were in control of the message because they were the primary resource that customers turned to in order to understand the selling organization's offerings.

Today, the customer has undoubtedly looked at your website (2.7 billion people are Net savvy), where marketing's ideas are presented before that customer ever talks to a salesperson. In addition, before interacting with you as the salesperson, customers have probably looked you up personally on social media sites like LinkedIn or Facebook and already made their judgments about you. Finally, if there is anyone in the world saying bad things about your organization, they have probably heard all of that too. In short, the salesperson has less and less control over the message.

But this change in information, and to some extent power, is bad news only for the "product pusher" salesperson—or the old "brochure" salesperson. There are literally busloads of salespeople of this variety still trying to operate in this new "connected" and "screen-based" world, but they are an endangered species. Their primary value used to be telling the customer about the company's products and services, but this is redundant now. The Internet does a better industrial job of getting information across. This means that *you*, the salesperson, need to bring something more to the table, something of value to the buyer that they could not get from the Net.

Adapt to Survive

Some salespeople have no problem with the change because they have always offered more than product-centric information. These are the top producing *solution sellers*. They are the salespeople who engage the customer at the highest levels and offer real insights during the sales dialogue. They are also wired to challenge their customers' thinking, to open their eyes to unrealized opportunities or issues that the buying organization had not seen or believed were resolvable. *Now* is the time for these people. They are the fittest for the niche, and they will excel in this modern role.

The best description of the role this type of salesperson plays is found in the book *The Challenger Sale*, by Matt Dixon and Brent Adamson. These authors do a great job of describing what the C-suite sale requires and how a Challenger salesperson meets those requirements.

To paraphrase their findings, supported by extensive study, the Challenger salesperson is a strategic thinker who knows enough about his products, customers, and the priorities of the C-suite, to have a business conversation of equals. In this conversation, Challenger salespeople can offer insights, make bold statements, and be relevant as advisors. They use these skills to activate triggers in their target clients for reviewing choices and initiating evaluations of options. These salespeople are also collaborators and consensus builders. They work within the buying organization to share their ideas, stimulate thought and discussion, and then rally the buying organization around an initiative. In short, they show up as trusted advisors, and everything they do in the sale reinforces that status until they have the credibility to lead a selection process.

The complex sale environment of the future (and many would argue the future is now) demands that the solution salesperson be a strategic-minded Challenger inside of target accounts. He must be able to take the messages of marketing, the results of a web search, and the buzz of social media and connect it all to the needs of the customer. His job is not to "show up and throw up" a lot of product detail, but to show up, show he understands and has information of value to customers by enabling them to achieve their business goals. The behaviors, habits, attitude, and processes of the very best salespeople in the past are becoming the table stakes for entry into complex sales in the future. To be one of these new breed of elite reps requires two things:

1. Understanding how to prepare for the key Power meetings
2. Understanding how to behave when you are in the key Power meetings

Chief of Concept

Strategic Selling, Advanced Selling, sometimes called Provocative Selling, is reserved for the boldest sales professionals. To be successful at it requires a combination of skills and attitude. These skills include a deep grounding in the fundamentals of senior executive level business management decision making combined with master level selling skills. The attitude begins and ends with the confidence that you belong in that room because you grasp executive issues as well as they do and can truly contribute to moving their thinking forward. This type of selling is not for the faint of heart, nor is it a place you can pretend. This is serious business and demands the discipline in your craft found only in professionals dedicated to the effort of bringing all the elements together.

The critical moment of a strategic sales cycle happens when the salesperson meets with the key senior executive. This meeting is not a sales call or a closing call—it is a *concept* call. Your understanding and governance of "time" here is a nonverbal key to displaying your understanding and allegiance to C-level values. There is no time in this meeting for long drawn out discovery; this is not where the salesperson asks open-ended questions hoping the executive will "share the pain." The salesperson shows up with a *hypothesis* that does things.

First, the hypothesis includes assumptions about the organization's current state based on deep and extensive research. The salesperson must be able to reach into relevant facts that reflect where the organization is right now. Second, the hypothesis should identify the root causes of any negative implications in the current state, and the salesperson must present this "root cause" positioning in a coherent and credible way, while at the same time in a calm and assertive manner. And finally, the hypothesis must propose a course of action that will remove or otherwise remediate the "root cause" to create an improved "future state." In the end it will all fall down, however, if the future state is not relevant to the goals, issues, and priorities of the executive's organization. A well-executed strategic call ends with support from the executive for the hypothesis and agreed-upon next steps to either prove the assumptions or prove the solution changes, identify the root causes, and support the future state.

Captains of Industry

Thinking back to our stick figures in Chapter 3, there cannot be any "sales stereotype behavior." This has to be two businesspeople sitting down to a business conversation about their two organizations and how they can work together. The salesperson has to achieve trusted advisor status from the outset.

How, you might ask, is this different from any other sale?

In typical sales cycles, either the salesperson has an "offering" (a solution) and seeks to trigger the buyer to want to look at it. Ideally this looking begins with the salesperson and the customer doing "discovery" (research) to determine *the fit* of the solution and its potential impact. Or more typically, the salesperson learns that the buyer has already initiated an evaluation, maybe choices, and the salesperson is now in with all the other vendors. Either way, the salesperson asks for the customer to dedicate her time and resources to work with him to determine if the solution is the right one for the organization to achieve its goals.

In a Challenger sale, to use the language of Dixon and Adamson, the seller has already completed most of the discovery before meeting the executive. He shows up with the business case—he's not showing up asking to build the business case. The call pattern shows the prospect, "This is your current state, right?" If the answer is yes, then, "This is what is causing this current state. Do you see it now?" If the answer is yes, then, "This is the desired future state and this is what should be done to get you from your current state to there, okay?" If the answer is yes then the Challenger can now facilitate discussions that start the Choices and Evaluation. The persuasive and influential structure that is being used to present here and build the business case we call the "PentaPoint," and it can be set out in the following way:

1. Where are we now?
2. How did we get here?
3. Where do we want to be?
4. How will we get there?
5. What will we do first?

Note how the structure takes the buyer on a physical journey. It is designed to *facilitate the buyer toward* embodying the situation so that the buyer can experience it and be *moved* by the story. The salesperson needs to be both assertive and collaborative in presenting this story. He needs to lead, but as a "partner," not a vendor. If you are going to meet a senior executive in a target client company in the hopes of creating a champion for your ideas, you have to bring that senior executive a business idea that helps her. And as such, this is a conversation that may never even mention your product, service, or offerings. This is a business conversation about the circumstances and opportunities for the customer's business as it tries to achieve the goals of its strategy. Unfortunately for most salespeople, this is one of the most difficult things to do. Why is this?

Dead Set

Everyone, not just salespeople, everyone—CEOs, CFOs, project managers, through to frontline customer service people—struggles with a phenomenon you can call *Product Bias*. Quite simply, the Product Bias is like a filter over your eyes that obscures your view of the world (a neural structure in your limbic brain founded on values that keep your behavior in line with your tribe). This translates into the allegory of hammers and nails—if all you have is a hammer, then every problem looks like a nail. In the context of the Product Bias, the hammer is your offering and the nails are your prospects. In other words, your offering is always the answer.

The way the Product Bias manifests itself in sales and sales planning sessions is that the selling organization answers every question with a description of how its product would help. There are two problems with this bias: first, it sounds salesy and bores the customer. Second, it tends to limit the seller's view of factors outside his solution; in other words, it tends to make it look like the answer is easy. At the executive level this draws suspicion because it demonstrates that the seller is just selling. The executive wants someone who can have a complete conversation about the company's circumstances and who does not bring out a solution until what really needs to be done has been described.

These conversations therefore require that you display the body language of someone who is *suspending judgment*, that is, you have suspended your product bias for now and are open to all inputs, view, and attitudes about the ways to proceed. Ask yourself: "What would someone who has no bias to your product do? How would that person behave?" Now do that! It may look like clearing the decks of all materials about your product or service, or taking the meeting in a neutral zone, well away from symbols of your offering. You will of course keep your nonverbal communication open, calm, and assertive—in the right starting place for your prospect to understand that you are there to perform critical thinking with her, rather than touting your preformed opinions about the fit of your product or service to the problem.

Ford's Three Simple Questions

In November 2004, in the gym of a hotel in Jacksonville, Florida, I learned a valuable lesson I will share with you that unlocks the key to every sales conversation and stands today at the center of our sales consulting practice. First some context:

1. There was a TV in the gym playing CNN.
2. It was right after the U.S. presidential election in which George W. Bush won his second term.
3. I am Canadian and was wearing a Roots Canada T-shirt with *Canada* across the chest.

Early in my workout session I decided to try the hotel's fancy bench press machine whose operation, in all honesty, had completely confounded me. There was one other person in the gym, a gentleman of 60 years or so, and he was kind enough to volunteer to show me how to use the machine. I thanked him and got to work on my sets.

A few moments later John Kerry, the loser in the election, appeared on CNN. The sound was down, as I recall, so I do not know what he was saying, nor was I much interested in it or his demeanor. Anyway, the friendly gentlemen who had helped me with the equipment turned to me and asked, "So what did you folks in Canada think of the election?"

If Mark had been with me, he would have seen my "freeze" response. Some of you reading this now might be Canadian, or at least know one or two Canadians, and therefore it should not shock you to hear me describe us as terminally polite, and in this case I tried to be no different. I quietly replied, in a neutral voice, not wanting to offend, "I guess we were not too worried either way." Ooops! This was pretty much the worst answer I could have offered.

The gentleman turned out to be a Baptist minister who proceeded to give me a 45-minute sermon on why this was the wrong answer! But the reason this event has stuck with me for so long is that the key fundamental principle the minister shared with me instantly became a cornerstone of my sales training.

He said, in all situations there are only three things that matter:

Why are we here? What is wrong? And what should we do about it?

This is a profoundly powerful set of questions, and it applies deeply to the complex sales model. If you consider for a moment that if you do not agree with the customer on why we are here and what is wrong, it is going to be really hard to agree on what to do about it.

With this attitude, you can bring them your analysis and the facts that support it. And here is the structured way to walk them through this challenge with executive presence:

1. What are you trying to do?
2. How are you doing it now?
3. What are the consequences of how you do it now?

And finally:

4. How would our offering dissolve some consequences?

Diving into the Deep

Researching the "what" answer should be the most straightforward. It can be found in annual reports, news announcements, speaking engagements by the executives, in company mission statements, or from industry research. The goal for your business case is to understand "what" the customer's strategic goals are, how those goals are measured, and what the obstacles are to achieving those goals. One of the reasons that many complex solution sellers choose "verticals" is that it makes it easier to understand what different customers in that segment are trying to do; your conclusions are more repeatable, and your cycle time between target identification and completed research is shorter.

Once you know what your buyers are trying to do, you can begin your research to find out how they do it now. What processes, tactics, and strategies are they deploying to achieve their goals? The best source of getting this information is often by contacting people inside the target company at the operational or management level—but *not* the executive. The idea is to get your facts as straight as possible before reaching up to the executive.

Your research is complete when you can answer the first three questions: *What are they trying to do? How are they doing it now?* and *What is going wrong because of how they are doing it?* The next step is to form a hypothesis grounded in the how they do it now and how they could do it. Again, as much as possible this hypothesis should not make specific mention of your solution; rather, it is focused on the *how*.

For example, if a prospect company was dependent on seeing specific information in order to make key decisions and that information today reached the decision makers via a paper report that was compiled at the end of every day, a consequence might be the timeliness of the information and the opportunity cost of the lag in that information reaching the decision makers so they could take action. If the prospect in this example said, "Yes, that is a problem," and then expanded on the answer with examples of decisions that were delayed by reliance on the paper report, which had a clear negative impact on the business, the seller is set up to create a "What if" answer: "What if that information was available on your tablet?" The buyer can now imagine what the implications would be if the information was available in real time. This should lead the buyer to ask the seller, "How would you do that?" Now the seller can bargain for proof, and understand how the buyer would evaluate a solution. "I think we can help, we should evaluate it, but assuming we can prove it, what would be the process your organization goes through to do that evaluation?" In other words, we now have agreement with the buyer on what she is trying to do, how she does it now, what goes wrong, and how a solution could change or eliminate the consequence and get to a more desirable result. The seller and buyer can now collaborate on how to evaluate if this answer is achievable and is as good as it sounds.

The above example is pretty simple, and it would usually take more than one or two solutions to motivate a large sale, but the point of the example is to show the value of getting agreement on the *What? How?* and *What's wrong?* before collaboratively painting the solution picture. Finally, all of this stage setting should be done as much as possible without mentioning the offering; in other words, avoid that product bias. You are discussing an idea here, not selling a product.

Having a Balanced Attitude

The more congruence there is between the gestures on both the left and right side of the body and any words that are spoken, the less chance there is of misinterpretation, confusion, or cognitive dissonance. For example, if you stand and place your hands symmetrically in the TruthPlane and say the words, "You can trust me," notice how steadfast and confident you appear, sound, and feel. Now place one hand in the PassionPlane and the other in the GrotesquePlane and notice a decrease in credibility, as well as physically, vocally, and psychologically, when you again say, "You can trust me."

Let's test this out further on someone close by.

To experience for yourself the amount of confusion you can create by using asymmetrical gestures (different gestures on the two sides of your body) that have no relation to your words, you'll first have to find someone to talk with. Look around; pretty much anyone will do. As you talk with this person, make sure your right and left hands are consistently at different horizontal levels. Furthermore, find as many moments as you can to change those horizontal levels. During this exercise, your hands should never be at the same horizontal GesturePlane. As you gesticulate in this way, see what happens to the expression of the person to whom you are talking. Notice how he relates to you both physically and verbally as a strong indicator of how well he understands the content that you are exchanging with him.

Because you have been constantly changing your gestures yet also keeping them asymmetrical, a huge amount of dissonance is created for your listener. No doubt you will have witnessed this confusion for yourself. Indeed, some of you will have noticed that the person with whom you were speaking actually took a step farther away from you (potentially showing an "avoid" response), and in some cases will have found a reason to exit from the conversation entirely. It is uncomfortable to be on the receiving end of a speaker who is using incongruent and asymmetrical gestures. However, not only is symmetry simpler and easier to understand in the body, but it also appears that humans prefer it and are more attracted to it.

Many psychological researchers now believe that symmetry is the secret to how we are attracted to form. Studies have shown that babies will spend more time staring at pictures of symmetrical individuals than at photos of asymmetrical ones. Among adults, it has been shown that when several faces are averaged to create a composite, thus covering up the asymmetries that any one individual may have, these composite faces are deemed more attractive by more people. And numerous scientists in the field of biology have found that the preference for symmetry is a highly evolved trait seen in many different animals. Females from swallows to swordtail fish, for example, prefer males with more symmetrical tails.

The bottom line is that research shows that beauty matters; just look at any magazine stand and the number of beauty magazines on offer. It is no secret that beauty in all its manifestations pervades society and affects how we engage with one another. Bearing in mind the impact of symmetry on how we are perceived, we can help an audience perceive us at our most attractive by practicing symmetry in the body when communicating, giving us a true business advantage. And if, for any reason, you should ever wish to be off-putting with your body language, go for asymmetry.

Here is an effective way to see how asymmetrical body language can work to your advantage when you are communicating. Imagine that during a presentation, when you are talking about your competitors, you use positive speech but asymmetrical gestures. You can add some very complex gestures, both asymmetrical and shifting across all the horizontal and vertical planes of gesture. How does using this asymmetrical and complex nonverbal language make you feel about the credibility of the competition? If you want your audience to steer away from the competition and go with your business, even though you may be using positive verbal language, you won't be selling it for your competitors. You will in fact be creating a feeling of confusion around their offerings.

Now imagine that when you are talking about the product or service you are promoting right now, you switch your body language to symmetrical gestures in the TruthPlane. Can you feel how your content is elevated above that of the competition in the minds of your audience, although you were using complimentary verbal language while discussing both? By using asymmetrical and complex gestures, you can easily cause dissonance around content that you want to devalue in the audience's mind, and by using simple symmetrical gestures, you can promote ideas in an audience's mind.

Baited

There are three distinct stages to this sales process: Research and Consensus Building, the executive meeting to gain Power Sponsorship, and using the sponsorship to lead the buying organization through the Evaluation process.

Research and Consensus Building is about reaching into the organization to validate your hypothesis, gain support for it, and prepare to meet the executives. This phase is a little different from a sales cycle initiated by the buyer (as we looked at in earlier chapters) in that there is no formal evaluation. As salesperson you must gain access to this tribe, inspire collaboration, and lead its members to a deeper understanding of their situation. The calls and meetings in this stage require you to register as a "friend" with everyone you contact. Your body language needs to be collaborative and authoritative: you are not trying to be seen exactly as an equal here; you want your various audiences to engage with you, but you want their perspective to be that they are talking to an authority figure—more than a trusted advisor, you are a subject matter expert for a specific business solution.

Now imagine you are in the target organization, having your meeting with your first contact, and that contact suggests introducing you to someone else. You and your contact head to the cubicle of the other person for you to meet. Adopt the attitude of the person introducing you. Mirror his moves as you approach and enter the territory of the person to whom you are being introduced. Use your body language to raise the status of the person you are being introduced to, and as the conversation begins to develop, find ways to be open, calm, and assertive in your nonverbal communication. The start of the introduction will most probably have a two-on-one orientation to it. See how quickly you can open the orientation to the "campfire" or "triad" setting discussed in Chapter 7 to create a sharing of status and rank, and build the feeling of a tribe.

Okay, your research is done; you have talked to a few people, built your consensus, found your sponsor, trust your facts, and you have your hypothesis: it is time to call or get a sponsor to set up the meeting with the big cheese! The average salesperson is terrified of going into the heat of the C-suite! Don't forget, the executive will smell fear! You will lose all credibility if your presentation is full of great ideas but is presented by someone who looks like a caged predator ready to jump the moment the bars are opened, or timid prey who knows he has ambled right into the "shark's cage." And to add chum to the water—these people are busy. Their time is valuable, and they and their organization cannot afford to waste it, so they may have little or no patience with salespeople making presentations from the product bias.

On top of all this, understand that many corporate cultures at an executive level do not openly use the language of problems, implications, or failure; they want to be seen to discuss opportunities, results, and success (even though their reptilian "problem/solution" brains can often be on high alert for threats and fixes). The first part should have come out of your research, and you use those insights to set the stage for a further conversation about alternatives.

Against the Clock

When this meeting starts, you have to be successful in the first three minutes or you will lose this audience fast. This means two things: you should rehearse your opening before the meeting, ideally with your sponsor in the buying organization that set up the meeting. The second is that you of course need to get your nonverbal signals in line to reinforce the message and establish your suitability. You are talking to this audience about its strategy; you have to look like you belong in the conversation and can deliver on the idea. The first piece is your responsibility. Now to the second piece: how to make sure your body language sets the right environment and helps achieve your goals of collaboration and authority.

Remember this checklist:

1. Be as *visible* as you can throughout the meeting: come out from behind furniture, computers, lecterns, coffee cups, pads and pens, and do not hide yourself behind furniture or props or behind your own limbs—uncross your arms and your legs and keep your hands away from your face.

2. Gesture predominantly in the TruthPlane: get your hands in open palm positions and your gestures in the horizontal plane that extends from your naval.
3. Keep balanced and *symmetrical*: keep your body and gestures as equal on either side of your body as possible. Keep your movements simple and uncomplicated. Be physically consistent: make your choice, make it bigger, and keep it tidy.
4. Be *predictable* and direct with your actions. *Slow down*, and move toward your objectives in a straight line.

All of these, as you know by now, calm your audience's primitive brain and allow the participants to open up their tribal brain to accepting you, and their logical brain to thinking through your thesis and proposition with an open heart and mind.

The Hive

Once the executive meeting is complete and you have buy-in from that Power Sponsor for your hypothesis, it will be time to prove that the solution can be delivered and will work. This will start to look like a regular complex sale evaluation except you will have a different status. In this case you should not look like an outsider trying to get in, but an inside advisor with sponsorship from the very top. This demands that your body language always engages, but also echoes that higher authority support.

Imagine you have a group of people in a discovery sales meeting. There are up to half a dozen representatives from the target organization. Your original sponsor is in the room from your consensus building effort, but the Power Sponsor is not. You, with the permission of your sponsor, will lead this meeting. And here is where some really powerful nonverbal influence and persuasion is going to come into play.

The members of the tribe are "anchored" (attached or triggered unconsciously) to their leader (the Power Sponsor) by that leader's nonverbal communication. And so it is the leader's nonverbal communication you are going to mirror in this meeting in order to borrow her status, rank, or authority during your messages. Now, you are not going to do this in a blunt and obtuse way with some kind of badly acted mime, pastiche, or impression of the leader, because you don't need to. What many in the world of influence and persuasion forget when it comes to what NLP might call "pacing and leading" or "mirroring," is that for people who have their brain correctly socially wired—that is, their limbic brain is fully functioning, as it is with the majority of social humans on our planet—they are already mirroring the leader. That's why the leader has accepted them.

So you are going to think about what you and your sponsor physically do when you meet together, and about whether your actions together are the same, similar, or resonant. Is there a speed and rhythm that you both adopt? Are there some specific gestures you both adopt? Is there a pattern of speech and tonality that you feel you both fall into together? Collect your thoughts and data around this, then decide which behaviors you can most easily control, and then concentrate on performing with these behaviors to the others in the meeting. You are finding the essence of nonverbal behavior. You are sensing and adopting the "archetype" of the group's tribal leader and have her "spirit" in the room with you. In this way you bring the power of the Power Sponsor into the space even without the sponsor being there!

Chapter 8 Quick Study

Complex sales are evolving to raise the bar for all sales behavior. The days of carrying brochures and talking product are going to end soon. As a salesperson in the B2B market, you need to do your homework, build up a broad business understanding, and then develop expertise in specific industries as they relate to the offerings you represent. With this foundation, you will then need to place yourself into the executive suite and behave as a native and a leader of the tribe. This evolution in the sales role is a great opportunity, but it will be an opportunity whose rewards are granted only to the most disciplined sales professionals who perform their craft with talent, skill, and deliberate practice.

Just Do This Now

1. In everything you do around presenting yourself at an executive level, including your nonverbal presence, answer the questions: *Why are we here? What is wrong?* and *What should we do about it?*
2. Present yourself with executive presence: be *visible*, in the TruthPlane, *symmetrical*, and *predictable*.
3. Mirror some nonverbal traits of your Power Sponsor that communicate her "essence" in order to communicate to others that you are conducting business with the Power Sponsor's authority.

Theory to Practice

In tests published in the *Journal of Personality and Social Psychology*, looking at what can be called "the chameleon effect," participants in an experiment who sat down to have a chat with an insider on the experiment were told to vary their mannerisms in systematic ways. Participants naturally copied the confederate—increasing some behaviors by an impressive 50 percent.

In the second experiment, the insider mirrored some of the participant's body language and behaviors. Afterward, participants were asked how much they liked the confederate. When the body language was copied, "liking" for the confederate increased almost 20 percent.

Finally, the participants filled out a self-assessment questionnaire about their empathetic abilities. And it was found that regardless of their individual beliefs in how empathetic they were—the levels of empathetic behavior remained constant across the sample.

So it would seem that it does not matter how soft-skilled we think we are—we *are* naturally designed to copy others and like people more who are acting like us.

Given this, what could this mean to your business? And what can you do about it immediately?

A Body of Knowledge

Paul Nazareth is a charitable gift planning specialist with Canada's largest philanthropic advisory team in the Scotia Private Client Group (scotiaprivateclient.com/philanthropy). He has spent more than a decade working in charities big and small and is a master and a passionate advocate of networking. Here he talks about creating nonverbal affinity with major benefactors in a way that can serve the whole community.

Fund-Raising Isn't Always Asking

Much like sales, the world of nonprofit and charity fund-raising can look all about "asking." Yet one of the key dangers to avoid is communicating with the body and tone of the "all the time ask."

Too many fund-raisers who have climbed the ranks of the world of special events to mail and online fund-raising forget to "turn it off" when they get to the role of "major gift" service. Often these people are overexcited, their body language always slightly aggressive and hands constantly darting into as Mark Bowden calls it the "PassionPlane." Which can be great when presenting to a large crowd, but not when sitting down for a casual lunch at a restaurant. Then, the questions became more like interrogations.

Instead, consider using those mirror neurons we are all born with. Meeting the donors where they are is a key to communicating for success in the leadership fund-raising business.

The best fund-raisers I have observed get into a state that is focused on listening and connecting. Their body language reflects this, leaning slightly forward but keeping hands in the TruthPlane, showing the donors that they are present and "with them." And time and time again I have seen that gestures toward the body in the TruthPlane when speaking about connecting values builds trust and affinity.

People want to do business and commit with people like themselves.

Leah Morrigan is Canada's first female men's image specialist and is completely fascinated with men, their behavior, and their clothing. She is in the business of building confidence and inspiring professionals, politicos, and everyday Joes to be the best that they can be (transformyourself.ca). Here she talks about the three quick steps to making a great first impression at an executive level.

Top Drawer

As Mark Bowden noted in *Winning Body Language,* congruence between words and body language wins trust, and this includes grooming and wardrobe. When our visual attire is not in harmony with our words and body language, our credibility can be compromised.

Try to become objective about your appearance, and don't be afraid to ask outside parties for their reading of you so you can get a sense of what you look like to others.

Tips for Sales Professionals

1. Before going on a sales call or meeting potential clients, research their corporate culture to understand their dress code and to mirror them. When in doubt, remember that it's better to be overdressed than underdressed.
2. Spend as much as you can on quality wardrobe pieces and be sure to have each piece properly tailored to fit you so you feel at your best and most confident. It will show.
3. Wardrobe details that communicate professionalism:
   - French cuffs and cuff links
   - Polished shoes
   - Pocket square/hankie

Remember, we have only one chance to make a first impression, and right or wrong, humans judge what they see.

Fire and Ice

Communication Technology and Collaboration

It will be the same online as it is around the campfire:
if you can't tell a good story, nobody will listen.

Mark Burnett

In this chapter you'll learn:

- New technology challenges your trust and credibility scores
- Nonverbal communication skills necessary for success on screen
- Insights on new media to give you a competitive advantage
- Screen-based setups to benefit your body language
- The secret skills of the top TV sales presenters

It is always easy to spot people who are new to video calling: they look at themselves with a combination of fascination, discomfort, and sometimes naked curiosity. This is fine, but it is not helpful if you are a salesperson—you need to appear less involved with yourself and more involved with your potential customers or clients and their issues. Some will lament about how video takes away a convenient mask that they enjoyed behind the telephone or e-mail. But those of you who understand how opening up channels that suggest a greater "exposure" to the client may prove to be an advantage will already be experiencing the benefits of communicating with your customers via the computer screen.

The key drivers of sales success—credibility and trust—as influenced by your body language are ever present on screen too. Based on this understanding, it is obvious that the techniques already discussed throughout this book are just as applicable to a screen-based environment. As with real face-to-face interactions, in virtual face-to-face meetings complexity increases as the amount of people involved in the communication increases. Yet in the face-to-face interactions talked about so far, we have kept proximity as a constant: always within public, social, personal, or intimate distances (anything from 25 feet to 6 inches). So now we are going to pull into focus the ever-increasing and more modern circumstance of communicating face-to-face but over distances that can be intercontinental, in many circumstances, within a global marketplace. This whole new layer of complexity that we need to deal with is both technical and psychological. Yet there are solutions to give you the competitive edge that are body based and powerful.

Increasingly, video broadcast is becoming available to salespeople, and it is a technology that really should be embraced. Why? Because like all good industrial tools, it offers significant opportunities to accelerate and increase the development of sales, and all for less cost. At the same time, video includes a number of risks that can potentially cause you more harm than good in achieving your goals; as with all technologies, there is a right way and wrong way to use it. This is great news because as video penetrates deeper and deeper into the communication practices of everyone, most salespeople who compete against you are never going to take the time (that you are taking now) to understand exactly how best to handle the tool. This means they will be making many of the technical and logistical mistakes (that you will avoid!) that impact the psychology of relationships, credibility, and trust negatively.

+ / Δ

You will most likely be familiar with company and product names such as Skype, Webex, Go-to-Meeting, Lync, Google Video Chat, and the video-conferencing offerings from Cisco and Polycom. All of these, in response to the inevitable penetration of video, have provided such communication wherever the Internet or other data connectivity dwells. If it has not arrived already, video is ultimately coming to your desktop soon, and in fact to all of your mobile devices as connection quality inevitably improves and deployment costs decrease. As a result, more and more sales communication is already being done with video. So this is a great time to get yourself prepared to excel with this medium.

Technology is fantastic when it works, but as anyone who has beat up his computer keyboard when faced by the fifth crash of his PC that hour can tell you: when it doesn't work, it is painful and frustrating! In the case of video calls, technology not working is a big, big problem. Why? Because the goal of a video call, particularly in a sales situation, is to allow you to pick up and respond to the visual communication cues of the other participants. To do this requires that the technology be almost "invisible." Yet, unfortunately with video, if the quality is low, the technology becomes all you see. For example, we all know from watching a poorly synchronized broadcast of a film that if a voice is out of sync with the picture, you become very aware of it and this disrupts the flow of the story. Often, live video communication makes the claim that the higher the technical quality of the connection, the higher the social connection. And this is true, but only to an extent. An extent that may shock you.

Video So Sharp It's Like You're Somewhere Else

Many of the video services are advertising video as the way forward to creating the opportunity to be there—without being there. But in a business setting, this is not as important an advantage as we might intuitively think.

Distance collaboration (including how we are able to sell over distance) has been an area of research for many years as organizations steadily increase their use of technology to support sales efforts. And as we discussed in Chapter 3—on tribes, territory, and proxemics—the distances between people really do matter. So the questions are: what *exactly* matters about distance over screen-based communication, and how can you win an advantage from knowing this?

Well, recent tests looking at how computer-mediated communication technology affects collaborating partners in the three areas of *cooperation*, *persuasion*, and *deception*, as used over distance, *versus* communication within the same geographic location, indicate that over long geographic distances parties are more likely to deceive, be less persuaded, and initially cooperate less with each other, as opposed to someone they believe to be in the same city. In other words, as a seller, the farther you are perceived to be from the buyer, the greater the disadvantage you have in a competitive sale. People like to buy local. It is an unconscious bias.

This is a daunting revelation, given that new technologies in communication are often in part designed and sold on the basis that they build engagement over distance. So it is important to understand as fully as possible exactly what is going on here.

Near and Far

The physical proximity of people influences collaboration: people located closer in a building are more likely to collaborate. Physical proximity increases not only the frequency but also the quality of communication among collaborators. It has been found in studies at MIT that in this respect, if you are farther than 30 meters from someone, you might as well be several miles apart. But does the amount of distance matter with computer-mediated interaction?

Of course, it is claimed that computer-mediated communication generates and regenerates community by bridging distances between people—and almost everybody who has a Facebook account would probably experience this as true. It has also been claimed that through computer-mediated communication, people can quickly find and develop commonalities between each other—and again anyone who has ever been part of an online user group or special interest forum will have personal experience that this is indeed true much of the time for many, many people. The benefits of social media are clear. But what the screen-based sales professional needs to understand is the negative effect on an interaction that distance has. As stated earlier, there are three ways that interaction might be affected by the distance between collaborative partners:

1. **Cooperation.** As the perceived geographical distance increases between collaborators, cooperation decreases and competitiveness increases.
2. **Persuasion.** As the perceived geographical distance increases between collaborators, their ability to persuade each other decreases.
3. **Deception.** As the perceived geographical distance increases between collaborators, their deception toward each other increases.

In short, the degree to which people bond with each other decreases as the perceived geographical distances separating them increases. Why is this?

Home Rules

Each of us partially constructs our self-image by associating with "our group," our tribe. The borders and similarities that bind members of a tribe can change over time, but in general people who live and work within a mutually recognized geographic area will perceive similarity, and therefore ascribe more positive values to each other than to people who live *outside* those geographic boundaries. This does not necessarily mean they *are* similar, simply that we come to view our cohort in a more positive light, and superior to others, quite possibly because we desire to be viewed by those same people as superior too. The weird logic being: the brighter the other people are in my village, the brighter I must be too! And this is all part of what in social psychology is known as the "Propinquity Effect."

Close to You

Propinquity (from the Latin *propinquitas*, "nearness") is one of the main factors leading to interpersonal attraction and engagement. It refers to the physical or psychological proximity between people. So propinquity can mean either a physical proximity and/or a kinship between people, as well as a similarity in nature between things ("like attracts like"). Therefore, we see how two people living on the same floor of a building, for example, have a higher "propinquity" than those living on different floors, just as two people with similar political beliefs possess a higher propinquity than those whose beliefs strongly differ.

Another propinquity effect is the tendency for people to form friendships, romantic relationships, or business alliances with those whom they encounter often. Occupational propinquity based on a person's career is also commonly seen as a factor in marriage selection. Workplace interactions are *frequent*, and this frequent interaction is often a key indicator as to why close relationships can readily form in this type of environment.

Now keep this idea of "frequency" in your back pocket because it is an important factor that we will use in order to counteract the negative effects of geographic distance in distance collaborations. Meanwhile, understand that propinquity can be about more than just physical closeness.

We're Always Bumping into Each Other!

Propinquity can also be about *access*: residents of apartment buildings who live near a stairway, for example, tend to have more friends from other floors than those living farther from the stairway. The more *exposed* you are to people, the more likable you become to them, possibly because your behavior becomes more predictable as more data is gathered about you than others, who are not so fully exposed. Remember that to the primitive brain that scans nonverbal behavior for threats and benefits, insufficient data causes a default to negative perceptions.

Daniel Kahneman, in his book *Thinking Fast and Slow*, supports this point too. He notes that familiarity breeds cognitive ease whether it is a person, idea, word, or object. "Good mood and cognitive ease are the human equivalents of assessments of safety and familiarity." Furthermore, it has been found in tests that through familiarity, the positive effects of propinquity can be increased significantly in as short a period as nine hours.

Yet one of the common assumptions around communicating over distance using an electronic medium is that once a communication channel is established, the immediacy of it (real time—just like face-to-face) gives communicators in the "virtual meeting room" an equal advantage as if they were really face-to-face. No one would dispute that technology effectively bridges physical distance, but experiments fail to support that it instantly supports a connection of trust.

We Have the Best People Over Here

It would appear that we might generally evaluate the skills of those near to us to be superior to the skills of distant others. It would also appear that being in the same city as others promotes feelings of similarity. And if people intuitively know they are disadvantaged by distance—that is, ill-equipped to influence a "remote" person to form a favorable image of them—they may stretch the truth to compensate.

It is an assumption that video provides more opportunity for persuasion and should engender more cooperation and truthfulness simply because it affords more visual and verbal cues from a person than written text or audio alone. But there is a growing body of evidence that questions the behavioral effects of video interaction, and it would seem that perceived geographical distance has a profound effect on "likability." However, the effects of distance can also change in proportion to the frequency of communication.

Stop by Any Time

The effects of distance are swiftly overcome through successive interactions over time. Although people initially cooperate less with someone they believe is far away, their willingness to cooperate increases quickly with multiple interactions. Let's look at nonverbal methods for bridging social status issues that are inherent in communicating from a distant geographic location:

1. Raise the frequency of that communication over a day long period. Instead of talking once, find reasons to sign off and then call back a little later to see each other and talk again, and again. The idea of being regularly interacted with, rather than a one-off now and then, will increase your familiarity, likability, and the sense that you are predictable.

2. Show in your environment an affiliation with the geographic area you are contacting. What can you show in the background behind you or during the conversation that is topographically similar to the client's location?

3. Show how your dress is aligned with the dress of the geographic location of the client and that it reflects the values of the tribe with whom you are talking.

Frequency, Fashion, and Fairness

If video communication could be as common an interaction as turning to someone in the same office ("swivel and talk"), then this could counter many of the negative consequences talked about so far. The opportunity of video is to build those everyday bonds; so if you are using video, maximize the effect by making the video a part of your everyday interaction with contacts and buyers. The more the buyer sees you, the more familiar you will become, and the more integrated the buyer will feel you are part of his world. This will create cognitive ease and help to build trust and credibility.

In the video, you also have the opportunity to dress as you would in your office, provided your office dress will not surprise your audience. If it is your home office, your pajamas are probably not the right choice. What we mean is that while you might dress in a suit and tie if you met face-to-face, this state of dress might look strange if you are video calling from your office. The simplest advice is to align your dress code with your audience, just as we talked about in Chapter 4 on selling to the tribe.

Talk Good

In 2008, Joseph B. Walther (Michigan State) and Natalya N. Bazarova (Cornell), in their study "Validation and Application of Electronic Propinquity Theory to Computer-Mediated Communication in Groups," established unequivocally that as communication skill increases, complexity of information decreases, bandwidth increases, and the perceived number of choices among channels decreases, the greater the amount of (1) psychological propinquity and (2) satisfaction.

Understand any of that? Well, this speaks to two issues in video communication about which you should be sensitive when planning how to use it to support your sales calls. The cited study above showed that the stronger your communication skills, the better you can do with any communication technology. The "bandwidth" speaks to the communication environment and the amount of information that can be shared through it. This moves through a scale from the best being face-to-face, through different video quality levels, past the audio of the telephone, and ends with text-based solutions like instant messaging and e-mail.

What the study proved was that there is a real risk in the propinquity and satisfaction of meeting participants who are using a lower bandwidth technology to join the meeting. This means that the experiences of people participating by video in a meeting that has other members of their tribe participating face-to-face are at risk. Those meeting face-to-face potentially may have an unfair advantage over those of equal status at a distant location. The same is true for audio participants in meetings where other participants are using video. For a salesperson this means, as the facilitator, that you need to take special care to bring those low bandwidth participants into the meeting interaction as much as is fair, possible, and practical.

Ford Goes to Sales School

On the first day of school in ninth grade I walked into my science teacher's classroom and sat at a desk toward the back of the room. In walked what I remember as a middle-aged man, but he was probably thirtysomething, and took a position at the front of the room behind a long platform. Behind him was a large blackboard the width of the classroom. After we pupils had settled in our seats, he turned quietly to the blackboard and drew freehand from where I sat what looked to be a perfect circle on the blackboard. The whole class was immediately transfixed; that teacher had our attention.

I am afraid that is all I remember, which is probably a partial explanation of how I ended up an arts major in college instead of a science major.

A friend of mine in the sales profession, one of the best salespeople I have ever known, would call this freehand circle a "parlor trick." The thing about parlor tricks is that to be done to good effect, they need to look spontaneous and have a significant impact; but the reality is they are not spontaneous and the impact is planned by the "trickster" in order to get a preplanned result.

Back then it looked effortless, but now I realize that this teacher must have spent hours and hours in a classroom in *preparation:* practicing how to draw that perfect freehand circle.

If you are going to be successful with video in supporting your sale, you should similarly practice in this environment until it is so natural, it looks easy. Like an actor in the mirror practicing the subtleties of how to deliver to an audience, make sure you work with this technology so you are communicating with confidence and not allowing people to think you may be a novice. If you look unprepared and anxious, they are going to read your body language as untrustworthy, so don't let newness to the technology impact your ability to connect and communicate.

Get the equipment up and running and prepare!

Lights, Action, Camera

Salespeople should pay special attention to the details of setting up the right environment for video communication. There is really no "in between" with these tools: they are either helping or hurting a lot. It does not matter the actual reasons why the tool fails or whose fault it is—the customer will always subtract from your credibility and that of your product and service around the communication breakdown—and it also does not matter what reason the salesperson tries to explain away the disruption. Take the time to test your systems in advance, and practice using them until you look comfortable, relaxed, and trustworthy, and you inspire confidence.

Set your camera up to show a full and comfortable view of your face. The obvious is to make sure it is not a half-screen; no one wants to talk to a "Kilroy Was Here" image. Try to make sure the camera is level with your eyes, since you want the buyers to be able to comfortably look *into* your eyes. Avoid having them looking down on you, or up at you. The first will lower your status, and the second will lower your customers' status by giving you height advantage via the camera angle. Finally, set the camera to simulate a feeling of being within your personal space. You need to look comfortably close, rather than either "in your face" or distant.

With the end result in your sights of getting a feeling of comfortable intimacy with the prospects or clients, consider where you place their incoming video image. Try to line the image up close to where your camera will be focusing on you. This way, at the other end it will feel like you are looking into the camera when you are in fact focusing on their video picture. This speaks also to one of the most unique characteristics of working with video: the greatest challenge is to avoid distractions. It is easy when speaking over video to find yourself looking at other items on your desktop, or watching your own self-view in the video feed. Make a concerted effort to focus on the other party. Imagine you are looking directly in their eyes. Encourage that sense of intimacy, and encourage them to look at you the same way.

Practice in self-display like you would with a mirror. Call a family member or colleague and practice getting comfortable with video. Just have a friendly chat, or role play a business call. The goal is to get to the point where you are as visually aware using the video as you are face-to-face. Here are some other technical details to take into account in order to best capture your nonverbal performance and your trust-winning behavior:

- **Microphone.** Learn how to adjust your microphone on your PC with whatever video application you are using. Each technology is different, so it is worth becoming familiar with how to make adjustments before you are in the middle of an important call and scrambling to find the controls.
- **Speakers.** Identify where the volume controls are and determine how to make adjustments on the fly.
- **Headset.** A good compromise solution that tends to have fewer volume control issues is to use a headset. The headset is like a closed environment; there is less to go wrong.

And finally . . .

- **Light.** If they can't see you, then you may as well just have a phone call!

What Your Face Discloses

Your audience needs to see your face to know exactly what you are saying! Audience members look at how the lips are moving in order to help them understand the exact words you're using and correlate this with the supposed meaning, getting a message that is congruent. If the message is incongruent, they will tend to go with what they see and use that to decipher what they heard, and they might well misunderstand or be confused.

Here's a lesson about head space for the sales communicator not only on camera but in real space and time:

Pants on Fire The mouth and jaw area of the head is the horizontal gesture plane of disclosure. If the audience members cannot see this area, they feel closed off, and therefore lack information. They can easily turn this feeling into the idea that the communicator is purposely withholding data, or, to put it bluntly, lying! Of course, it is not necessarily true that the sender of a message with his hands in this area is lying (to work that out would take far more evidence), but that is often the feeling we get when someone speaks to us with his hands in this horizontal plane.

The lesson here is: keep your hands away from your mouth so that everyone can hear your meaning correctly. Conversely, you can use your hands up around your jaw and at mouth level to funnel the audience's vision toward your mouth and direct it to your speech. This would be a gesture of disclosure, seen as, "I am telling you everything." Try out this gesture for yourself: bring your hands up to your mouth level and use them to funnel an imagined audience into seeing the mouth area. Can you recognize how it quickly begins to feel as though you are imploring the audience to understand or believe you? You can also probably feel how quickly your energy (physical and mental) rises and becomes quite excited and frantic. Can you feel how your words might run away with you?

On the whole, gesturing around the lower face is to be avoided unless you wish to create a potential feeling of mistrusting the message. For example, try saying this with your hands in the DisclosurePlane: "I have given you our best price today." Remember that we believe what we see, so if you are covering the message, we are not as able to believe it. So now try the same sentence with your hands in the TruthPlane. You will instantly understand both the merits and the disadvantages of the DisclosurePlane from this exercise, and get a feeling for how using it—especially unknowingly—can create intense distrust in your customers or clients.

Read My Lips

To test just how much your audience relies on seeing your lips move to understand oral language, try this out on a colleague: chat with him and find ways to keep your hands over your mouth throughout. Notice how many misunderstandings occur and how frustrated your colleague gets because he cannot get the message since he cannot see the message. Now bring your hands down to the TruthPlane and note the relief in his face and body. He can now read your lips and see your intention in your face (as well as being assured by your gestures from the part of your body that engenders the most trust).

You may think that even the most naive sales communicator would not cover his face when he was speaking; however, you will notice, especially in long meetings at tables, that when the head gets tired (it weighs about 8 to 12 pounds, and the neck can get tired of carrying it), even a seasoned communicator's hands can easily creep up to the chin and the mouth to cup the head with elbows supported on the table to take stress off the neck, which is comfortable for the person holding her head up but very uncomfortable for the people who are trying to understand and communicate with her because they cannot see her words!

As ever, check out the performance of TV news anchors: when do they ever bring their hands up to cover their face when reading you the day's important news?

Chapter 9 Quick Study

The use of video in the sales function will continue to grow. Many people will assume, as with other technologies in the past, that they can take old habits into the new medium seamlessly, but achieving that will require dedication and practice. You will be able to differentiate yourself and your product or service from competitors in the market by working now at getting great with video.

There are risks and a variety of ways to get in trouble, so let these risks bite your competitors while you do your homework, so that not only do you avoid the same mistakes but that you use your communication skills to give your buyers an experience that separates you from everyone else by dealing intelligently with all the consequences of using this technology.

Just Do This Now

1. Work on building a stable video setup and environment and start practicing with it.
2. Make more video calls more often, especially to a new prospect.
3. Always appear via screen-based communication, just as you might if you were in the client's office visiting him. And just as you would do face-to-face, keep your hands away from your mouth.

Theory to Practice

Familiarity breeds . . . engagement!

Think about all the reasons in an office environment you can "pop by and say hi!"

"Did you see the game?"

"Get that e-mail I sent?"

"You'll never guess what I just heard?"

"Do you want to grab lunch?"

"I've got those details you needed and thought I'd just stop by with them. Got a moment?"

Now what is stopping you from doing this with your clients via video link?

Of course there may be some important cultural or logistical barriers, yet in some cases you could be acting more local even though you are in fact global, and winning more sales in the process.

Make a point today of acting local with one of your more distant prospects and see what happens.

A Body of Knowledge

James Lavers is the world's foremost expert in on-camera communication that gets the attention and action of your viewers. His Video Psychological Operations (vidpsyops.com) is the methodology of choice for celebrities, gurus, and corporations that sell on screen and want to be better believed and bought from via television or video. He has coached people like Anthony Robbins, Paul McKenna, and Wayne Dyer. Here he talks about making the first impression count on camera.

Video Psyops

With video and TV, your audience can click away in a cold second. So it's crucial you rivet your viewers' attention in the first few seconds. Here's how:

Mark Bowden's "symmetrical open gesture from the navel" is taught as standard operating procedure on my Video Psychological Operations course. Its trust-building power works when used in the opening seconds of any video, and for my $5000 a day clientele, we add something extra.

It's called the "friendly predatory gaze."

Do this. Look directly into a mirror. Stand tall and upright. Now, remaining upright, drop your chin two inches toward your chest (about the length of your thumb) while maintaining a steady, even gaze. That's a predatory gaze, commonly used by mammals that organize themselves into hierarchies of dominance, such as wolves, lions, and some primates. Look at someone of the same sex like that for a while and they'll begin to get seriously freaked out. So to make it less threatening while retaining the "alpha" authority this expression bestows, we add three special ingredients.

1. First, turn your whole body at a 45 degree angle to the mirror, but keep the measured, predatory gaze. Okay, now you are not head-on—you pose less of a threat (hard for you to pounce at that angle!)
2. Next we add something really special. A smile. Feel it.
3. Finally. Breathe, for goodness' sake. This stuff doesn't work if you're uptight—and the quickest way for that to happen is if you don't regularly and rhythmically inflate your lungs!

Now put it all together. Open gesture from the navel with a smiling, offset, predatory gaze and just say: "Hi, my name's [insert your name here]."You're in! That's the first few seconds and most of the hard work done . . . way to go!

Janine Harris (keyringmedia.com) is a producer, director, and editor with a passion for telling stories. With over 15 years' experience developing and producing for commercial, television series, and documentaries, she brings broadcast skill and technique along with web and new media strategies to telling the stories of business. Here she talks about how to rig your sound and lights to realize the best results from your screen-based relationships.

Son et Lumière

Most people tell me that when it comes to engaging in screen-based business communication, they can often overlook poor picture but if they can't hear it or understand what is being said, they'll tune out and check into something else.

When using a home video camera or computer, usually it's got a built-in microphone. To ensure that these cameras are effective for most uses, the microphones are designed to pick up as much of the sound around the camera as possible. Great if you are at your kid's soccer or a concert, or have the whole family around the PC Skyping with Grandma and Granddad. But if you are trying to make a video presentation and all your viewer hears is a big echoing room, or your neighbor's dog, or the hordes of people in the convention center, then that may not make the impression you'd hoped.

If you are shooting sales video with a home camera, or video conferencing with a laptop, here are a few ideas to get the very best from your setup:

- Pick a quiet space with lots of furniture and carpeting (to keep down the echo) but make sure the backdrop suits your presentation.
- In busier locations, keep the camera as close to you as possible. It may mean that you only see your face, but it will also keep your voice as the main focus.
- Whenever possible, try to use a separate microphone. I personally like a small lapel microphone that clips onto your shirt. It's designed to pick up audio all around (omnidirectional), but it works within a close proximity so you don't pick up all the noise in the room.

So if you are looking to purchase a camera for an upcoming video project or buy a new laptop for screen-based communication, pick one that allows you to connect an external microphone.

When it comes to lighting—less is more. Our instinct is to point every desk light at our faces so we will have the spotlight, but that isn't always the best solution, as it can cause harsh shadows. So before I look at adding any extra lighting, I first look at the environment. Where is the most light in a room, or where are the windows where there's lots of natural light? The easiest way to light yourself is to find one of those two scenarios. If you have lots of natural light by either being outside or with lots of windows, position yourself facing the window, then use a big piece of white cardboard to bounce light onto your face and erase any shadows that may be introduced.

Inside, we often deal with different types of lighting, like fluorescent or tungsten (regular bulbs). These two light sources actually change the color our eyes see on camera, so it's ideal to choose one or the other. Fluorescent is usually cooler (blue), and tungsten gives a warmer glow (red). Remember, always face your light source, and avoid light from behind, as that will inevitably make your face dark.

And while you are considering your environment, remember that viewers will always be looking at context, so while I discourage standing right against a plain wall (think mug shot), I also caution about too much stuff in the background—keep your viewers focused on what you have to say. Pick your environment to suit your subject matter, and if you're only option is to shoot in your office, take a good look around at what's going on in the background—is your office clean, are you showing confidential client information, are there family photos in the shot, awards, your library, or pieces of art? Look at everything and make sure it matches the message you want to communicate.

10

Sales Intelligence
Managing the Technical Mind

*Someone told me that each equation I included in the book
would halve the sales.*

—Stephen Hawking

In this chapter you'll learn:

- As the "technical resource," how to reinforce the right message
- Ways to best interact with your technical resource in the sales call
- What to do if you are technically leading the meeting
- Body language for the professional "rainmaker"
- How to use the "YesState" to manage stressful sales situations

People are stubborn and we all get set in our ways, so it's no wonder we want to believe some of the popular business psychology that suggests our inclination toward either creativity or organized thinking is decided at birth. You will have no doubt heard time and time again about "right brain" versus "left brain" thinking, and the idea that "left-brained techies" are no good at the "soft skill" stuff. All they can do is fulfill a version of their genetic destiny by being introverted eggheads who either enjoy basements and *World of Warcraft* or write long and incomprehensible algorithms on the windows of universities while failing to form any kind of meaningful human relationship. Some commentators say we should accept as unchangeable our strengths and weaknesses.

Under this regime it is so easy to assume, dictate, and support the idea that technical people only want to be "correct" and tell the truth, the whole truth, and nothing but the truth, and that those of us in sales need to be "creative"—make up some "stories" with distorted and deleted data to persuade clients to buy. Assuming these two opposing views or value bases can lead a number of technical people to feel out of place in sales situations, causing some to communicate in an uncomfortable way. And it follows that many sales professionals can be led to fear, resist, or outright refuse taking technical experts into a sales call because they are convinced that a techie's antisocial demeanor will "annoy the client and screw up my deal!"

It's Like Comparing Desflurane with Propofol

It is easy to see the sales professional as inhabiting the realm of the smooth talking extrovert, being the life of the party; that work hard/play hard person with no fear of strangers, and the ability to make anyone feel comfortable. And while this stereotype may or may not be true, the world of sales is certainly dominated by people who appear socially comfortable and enjoy working with others, as in, "He's a real people person!"

Meanwhile, technical experts who are so often essential (or in some people's minds a "necessary evil") to closing a complex sale are often seen as inhabiting a world dominated by loners and know-it-alls, either so inside their own heads that they can't communicate at all—and bore you to bits, sending you to sleep—or so self-assured and full of their own gas that you wish they would please stop speaking. Unfortunately, many of these technical resources find themselves in aggressive sales situations, either as the "answer person" for tough questions or, in many smaller companies, as the lone salesperson themselves. (Indeed there are plenty of examples of successful technical experts building tech companies and initially handling every role that the business can throw at them. And plenty of examples of how these individuals failed ultimately to sell their innovations, causing the company to bomb.) However you look at it, it is easy to recognize how the pressure of a sale could quite easily cause the best of us to clam up or come out all-guns-blazing (flight or fight!).

Λερναία Ύδρα

The technical person in a sales situation takes many forms: the software developer presenting the application to the buyer for the salesperson; a technical entrepreneur who has invented a better mousetrap and now needs people to buy it; and a professional, like a lawyer, thrust into the role of rainmaker for her firm. And all of these professionals share one thing in common, the refrain, "I am not a salesperson" or "I don't want to look or sound like a salesperson here." And rather like the experts in hardware stores who, when you ask, "What tile would look the best for my kitchen?" say, "It is totally up to you," this can be an annoyance. For many sales pros and clients, if you are not here to help, assist, or sell, what the heck are you here for!

Well, here is help. The goal of this chapter is to assist technical people in nonverbal communication techniques: how to survive, thrive, and become a trusted ally (rather than a misunderstood misanthrope) to the client. This will help you and your sales team as a whole in the sales situations you find yourselves in: Support, Presenter, Entrepreneur, and Rainmaker.

Support

The most common technical role in complex sales is the technical resource assigned to a salesperson to answer the detailed questions of the buyer. The technical resource should be primarily a proof resource; although, in some circumstances they are needed at the discovery phase too.

Discovery

The discovery call, also known as the "needs analysis call," is the step after qualification. In these calls of the complex sale, the buyer and seller have agreed to review the requirements of the buyer in more detail in order to help her understand the situation and new possibilities. In these types of calls the focus is on the buyer's current state, with an eye to identifying constraints in that state that are impediments to the business achieving its goals. A well-run discovery call will explore the current state in depth and then define a future state that will be made possible through the selection of the seller's solution and the collaborative implementation of that solution. Discovery calls are found in both the Choices and Evaluation stages of the buying process.

Discovery calls often include multiple parties from both sides of the buying decision, and here the technical resource is a second party on the sales side. In addition, as the sale moves forward there will often be multiple discovery meetings. Within this process the seller is not just trying to understand what the customer needs, but how the buying organization makes a decision. The latter calls for acute awareness of the people and their positions within the buying process. It also creates the opportunity for the seller to enter the tribe.

The discovery should be driving a deep sense of collaboration between buyer and seller. The more value the seller can add to helping the buyer see her situation and understand her opportunities, the more likely that seller can achieve the desired "Trusted Advisor" status. The goal of the technical resource is to substantiate the Trusted Advisor status of the salesperson. Imagine it this way: the buyer should walk away from a discovery event with a salesperson and technical resource thinking, "Of course that salesperson can guide us through these decisions; just look at the resource he brought for us today and how that resource validated us and our sales partner!"

The discovery call can easily be classified as the most critical event of the entire sales process. Done well, these events set the tone for everything that happens afterward. It is a great time to start collaborating because the focus is all about them, the buyers and client company as a whole. Get inside the tribe, gain status, be credible, add value, and build yourself into the trusted advisor here with a Power Sponsor, and it will be a lot easier to navigate the final stages of the buying process. If the sales team includes a technical resource, then the salesperson and technical resource should *synchronize their body language* to help both of them enter the customer's tribe. You know you have done this well when the buyer asks for the technical resource to manage the implementation.

Technical Resources in Discovery The goal of the discovery call, as described, is to explore deeply the buyer's current state. The technical resource can be a key participant in this discovery process. Often such resources are the best suited to have a deep discussion with the buyers about their current state. This is absolutely perfect, but there are some issues that can arise.

As a salesperson, it is important that you work with and rehearse your body language plan with the technical resource. This is to ensure that if you have two technical people in the room (your resource and that of the client company's) and one salesperson, the situation does not turn into two insiders and one outsider, which it can very quickly. While it is excellent that the technical resources from each company can be on the same page, if the salesperson becomes marginalized, this can potentially kill his status, and so severely hinder his ability to build and strengthen a relationship with the client company. The technical people are part of a tribe as well, and the technical selling resource needs to make sure to include the salesperson in his or her nonverbal communication.

This may feel like a tough demand for some technical people, especially if they do not think much of salespeople in general, and this salesperson in particular. Organizations would benefit from screening their sales supporting resources to ensure they can be inclusive of the salesperson, and vice versa.

The goal of the technical resource in the discovery phase is to raise not just their status, or their company's status, but the salesperson's status too. The idea is to help the salesperson attain the status of trusted advisor, and not have that status usurped by the technical resource. Imagine the following.

A salesperson and technical resource are presenting to a single buyer. The buyer is technically proficient, maybe it is a Chief Technical Officer (CTO) and this is a technology sale. The conversation quickly runs to questions and answers that only the technical people can answer. This creates a challenge because there is not a lot for the salesperson to say. But the technical resource should include the salesperson as much as possible. The technical resource should think of the conversation as a hot potato—she wants to end what they are saying and turn it back to the salesperson as soon as possible. And she can clearly signal this by turning as far as possible toward her sales partner on the call, allowing the client or customer to understand unconsciously that the sales professional still has status in the room and is an important player in the conversation—even if technically he hasn't a clue about what exactly was said!

This helps create a call pattern in which the salesperson is still summarizing points and managing the segues in the call. Another way to accomplish this is to have a simple overarching context to the discussion: for example, your company might be *the* company for customer service, and you believe the key to customer service is based on fast turnarounds when answering questions, deep domain expertise to enhance the completeness of the answer, and consistent follow up to ensure that the answers ultimately solved the problem.

The way a salesperson can manage the segues is if one of these dimensions is the common jump-off point for the deeper discussion the technical resource is having. This way, when the technical resource finishes her point, she can turn the conversation back to the salesperson by connecting the point just made back to the high-level context. Now the salesperson can pick up the cue and reinforce the point that was made and why it matters in the decision the customer is making. With the next question, the salesperson can again turn to the technical resource and repeat the process.

This call pattern raises the status of the salesperson and keeps him engaged in the conversation. It has the added benefit that the salesperson is well positioned to manage the progress of the call toward the sales process objective of the meeting . . . something that is almost impossible to do if the salesperson is sitting as a spectator to the conversation! And you know what that would look like: positioned outside the close phase of the social distance (more than seven feet) from the technical tribe, body too relaxed, body and head often turned away from the conversation, lack of eye contact with the customer and technical resource when they are speaking with each other; looks of anger, disgust, or contempt when the technical resource is speaking. Instead we need to see an engaged tension across the body, the body open and turned into the direction of the conversation, a light smile on the face when others are talking, along with a slight nodding of the head—remembering all the time, "My friend is amazing!"

Proof Presentations

The Proof Presentation refers to anything the sellers are presenting to the buyers to support that they are the right solution to enable the customer to achieve the vision created in the discovery process. This can take the form of demonstrations, customer reference visits, facility tours, and any other event that brings multiple people from the buying and selling organizations together.

These presentations can include multiple participants from the selling side and can include cooperative joint presentations with other participants, either vendor partners or even employees of the buying organization. In other words, they can look a lot like three-ring circuses. The more complex the situation, the more critical it is that you get all participants on the same page and orchestrate the event. This means you have to sit down for a clear conversation beforehand on the goals of this meeting, the parts you need to play individually, and how you are going to work as a team to achieve that result. And of course this means you are going to plan the physical operation of looking, acting, and behaving as a team—not only with each other but with the customer.

These events can be in a few different spaces: boardrooms, meeting rooms, occasionally theater/classrooms, and even be moving events in the case of tours and customer references. In some cases you could find yourself wearing overalls at an industrial facility, or even more robust protective wear at a secret desert test site! In all these cases there are many moving parts that the alert salesperson will be sure to choreograph to support all the principles discussed throughout this book.

Technical Resources in Proof

The different types of presentations discussed in Chapter 7 are made during Proof, but the ones most likely to include technical resources are often boardroom presentations. In these scenarios, the technical resource will probably have to "drive" part of the presentation, particularly around the details of how the solution would actually solve the customer's problems. This likely needs to be contextualized into the experience of the customer.

There are a few risks with a technical resource at the lead of a proof demonstration. Many organizations do not dedicate technical resources to full-time sales support; they are often a borrowed resource, taken from their regular duties of overcoming obstacles and troubleshooting problems inherent in the technicalities of the product or service being sold. This can lead to the "trainer" syndrome, where the technical resource presents to the buyer as a trainer, which is usually not a productive arrangement. It of course lowers the rank or status of buyers by placing them in a context of a "lack of knowledge." This is not training, and should not look like training. It should be a collaborative environment. How can you help?

Of course, if the technical resource is not accustomed to leading interactive discussions and is a "teller" by nature, then some intercession is required by the salesperson. Ideally, the salesperson and technical person would work together in advance to get the "drill" down; if there is no opportunity in advance for this type of preparation, the resource can be put in a position of being questioned by her own team leader and seeing her rank lowered in front of the new tribe (the client company). This risk is now fight-or-flight: the technical resource clams up or comes out all aggressive and arrogant.

In these situations, the better choice is to try to work with the physicality of the situation to make sure that you—the salesperson—can orchestrate the event from the sidelines with body language and nonverbal communication. Remember, the whole point of the training in this book is to help you control the environment in order to control the psychology and thus the outcome of the sale.

Consider this scenario:

The technical resource has had a lot of sales training, especially using *Winning Body Language for Sales Professionals,* and can easily use great nonverbal communication to support the feel of an interactive environment and move the meeting away from a lecture. In order to mitigate loss of status around a lack of technical knowledge on the part of the customer, the resource might take the meeting away from the boardroom tables and sit in a more casual interactive environment, perhaps like the U-shape (Presentation positioning) facilitative environment described in Chapter 7.

The resources could have the body language of their "coach" persona—alert to the customers' views, forward and interested when they speak, displaying open body language to the answers they give. They look to be listening more than telling—head to one side and nodding gently. The resources share technical materials with the client as they go through figures or diagrams, instead of a scenario where the client sits behind a desk with the "school books" being tested by the technical expert.

And now consider this one:

The technical resource does not do sales meetings often and has not had any training around *Winning Body Language for Sales Professionals.* As the salesperson, you will set up with the technical resource in advance on how you will handle the environment. As the technical person speaks during the meeting, you as the salesperson can insert yourself to the edge of the sightlines of the key decision makers. You are now in a position to intercept a question and shape it for the technical person, because many questions might have a deeper and more important relevance to the customer than the technical person will be able to see. For their part, technical people might have a tendency to accept a question at face value and start to answer. They can end up talking ad nauseum around fixing the presenting problem rather than addressing the real issue that provoked the question. Often, technical experts see themselves as part of a "doctor/patient" relationship and constantly try to save or heal the customer's surface problems with their medicine. This can feel aggressive, arrogant.

If you want to know how that aggressive doctor behavior might appear, just think now on the most annoying doctor you ever visited and how he physically and vocally came across to you. Now think about the most help-ful doctor you have ever visited. How did she greet you? What did she do with you? What was her rhythm of movement? What was her cadence or musicality of speech? And what was the impact of all of this on you? This is a clue as to how a technical expert can act to get the best out of some-one who needs help making the right decision. And you can help your technical experts perform in this way too by getting them to think of this annoying doctor/helpful doctor imagery and getting them to physically (and vocally) perform their part as "helpful doctor" during meetings and presentations.

The great salesperson knows to be less of a doctor, more of a coach. The salesperson knows that many questions should be answered with a ques-tion that gets deeper to the roots of what is being asked. For this reason the salesperson should, as much as possible, be prepared to step in (calm and assertive) and expand the source of a question as needed. This means that the body language of the technical person should always show a strong direction toward the salesperson. Note that this is not out of some ego-driven demand for control, but because the role of the salesperson is to manage the process of getting the customer to decide to buy. The pres-entation is an important element in the process, but the salesperson must maintain the authority to move the customer forward after a successful presentation. If the presentation robs the salesperson of status, then it has not helped the process.

Smells Like Team Spirit

Technical resources are incredibly valuable in the complex sale. The trick, though, is for them to work together with the salesperson to choreograph their body language and the nonverbal environment to persuade and influ-ence the buying process. The goal of these interactions is to raise the con-fidence of the buying organization in the selling organization. Buyers will judge the latter on how the salesperson and technical resource work together. Use the principles in this book to make sure your nonverbal communication does not contradict the words of unity and team spirit you are selling.

If possible, most organizations and sales teams should try to practice and rehearse their sales presentations together so that the interplay between them is seamless and helps inspire confidence. Like any tribe, they should spend time eating and playing together in order to unconsciously strengthen the bonds of trust. This *does* mean beer, pizza and bowling, paint-balling, Latin dancing, go-carting, pool parties, Twister, Buckaroo, and Jenga at the winter holiday party, or whatever you can think of that is *physical* and achievable by everyone once a quarter.

Trust is gained through groups monitoring each other's physical behavior over time, and especially in crisis. Games (ludic behavior, or "play") are one of the ways we achieve this drama theatrically or virtually, that is, without the risk of having to actually have a *real* crisis. It is essential for the members of any team to have times when they get to physically experience each other, as this will trump any intellectual experiences they have when the pressure is on. They will have fully sensed (seen, heard, smelled, and tasted) the strength of the team and will trust in the pleasure and security of being a part of this tribe. Equally so, you might immediately see the benefits of inviting a key client, or a prospect or two, to this kind of regular, casual team event, to bond them together with the whole crew.

Technical as Salesperson

Technical people end up in sales roles for generally two reasons:

1. They hit it out of the ball park as entrepreneurs with a great idea and suddenly find themselves in the new role of salesperson.
2. They have supported enough salespeople to feel they can do it too.

The instinct of technical salespeople is often to try to share everything they know. It is hard for them to resist the urge to speak from the product bias. This is especially true of technical entrepreneurs: it's all about the great new mousetrap!

So if you consider yourself a technical person in sales, you should consider using the knowledge and techniques in this book to slow yourself down a little bit. Stay in the TruthPlane and centered in the DoorPlane—calm and assertive. Do not overtalk the solution or your technical knowledge so you intimidate your audience. Your posture always needs to be inviting and engaging—open gestures, head tilted just a touch to one side, nodding gently now and again, and a light smile on your face. Practice listening. Learn to ask questions and listen for the answer. Use your body language to create patience in your listening. Think of the people you know who you believe really listen well. Study their nonverbal communication and mirror that.

Clients need to trust your physical behavior as well as trust your words and knowledge: it is by presenting this total package of how you hold yourself that you will earn their trust, and not just with words and demonstrations of knowledge.

Bring in the Rainmaker

There is a changing of the guard in many of the old professions, like law firms and accounting practices. The old "rainmakers"—the partners in the business who traditionally generated new business by finding ways to connect with people in the market—are handing the reins to a next generation, and for many of these new partners the notion of selling and rainmaking is a foreign concept. They see sales as something dark and beneath them and believe the customers feel the same way. But that does not change the need to generate clients.

The ubiquitous circumstance for a rainmaker is of course social engagements, like a cocktail party or industry networking event. For many professionals, these two circumstances can feel very awkward, and it shows. Here are some thoughts that can help.

At the "casual meeting," not everyone is a natural extrovert, and it is all right if you are not one either, but you can still be successful by leaving the right impression to begin a relationship which will ultimately be a successful business relationship. The key is to understand the situation and then use the TruthPlane to manage the impression you make in that situation.

The situation is: the other participants feel the same as you do, a little cautious, feeling a bit out of their comfort zone. The reality is that almost all of them want to be in a conversation, at least in an interesting conversation. Yet sometimes they just don't know how to start one. For many, a large casual meeting setting is a threatening environment. Our bodies want to freeze and then want to hide.

This reaction, as we've already seen, physically realized, puts you in the category of "indifferent" for others, and for some bullies makes you akin to "prey." It creates a posture that will inspire people to stay away, or for a very few to pick on you. Scan the floor of a trade show for displays of these natural instincts, and you'll see how often the people in a trade show booth and in the aisle want to talk, but their body language drives them apart. Or in some cases those perceived to be weak have been pounced upon in a conversation they do not want to be a part of, which will not lead to a sale of any sort. The predator has found easy prey rather than finding the bigger, healthier animal or pack that he really needs to track and befriend in order to get the resource out of them that his company needs in order to survive.

To be successful at a casual meeting, think back to Chapter 6 and the retail sale. Success in these circumstances is about opening yourself up and being approachable and nonthreatening.

Imagine you are mingling for cocktails at the end of the first day of a three-day industry event. You do not know anyone. You are nursing your drink. (Not building up liquid courage, but rather you are now in the room ready to meet people.) Have your drink at belly height—in the TruthPlane. Have a gentle smile on your face and use this tool: accept everything.

How exactly do you "accept everything" with your body language, you might ask? Well, it is pretty simple, and the effects are astonishing. You must put yourself into what you can now call the YesState.

Remember, the human mind is naturally programmed to assign a negative perception to anything that is unknown: this is a primal survival mechanism. And this perception is reflected—it *shows*—in your body language when you come across an unknown entity; for example, somebody in business who is new to you, or even somebody whom you know but who has a new idea. Even somebody who is known to you and has a known idea that merely has some element of unpredictability about it will be met by our primitive brains with some element of negativity. Instantly your brain goes, "Uh-oh! Oh, no!" and alerts you to a potential problem within the interaction, and this alarm frames the whole communication.

When you respond to an idea or a person in a way that gives you pause, your audience can see the elements of resistance in your body without your having to say anything. (Remember that potentially 55 percent of the feeling that people have about another person's intentions is based on what they see, and they can detect every nuance of movement, tension, and rhythm in the other person's face and body unconsciously.) When you are resistant to a new person or idea, that person can tell something is wrong, but he is left to wonder what the problem is: is it the way he looks, his ideas, what he said, or how he carries himself? It does not really matter, because your body language says that you don't accept him, and so for you, there is an instant drop in his status. And a perceived drop in status will most likely cause him to either withdraw or attack.

Either way, at a subliminal level you are no longer on ideal terms with your audience in the meeting, presentation, speech, or casual drink setting. You've lost your listeners, or even worse, if you are compelled to be aggressive toward them, they now mirror that, and feel aggressive right back toward you. That is a result of what you can call a "NoState"; this is our default state for most of the interactions we have. It's not a bad thing; indeed, it saves our lives on a daily basis. But it does not move us forward; it is simply trying to keep us stable. It does not allow us to take an opportunity by dealing with the risk in an intelligent manner.

The YesState™

In order to get into this nonverbal state of acceptance that can display a positive message to audiences of any size and help get a good conversation going at a cocktail reception, we are going to take on a mental attitude of acceptance and positivity. However, there is no great psychological preparation for this, only to review as much positive verbal vocabulary as you can think of. Here is some to get you started:

> Yes/okay/good/agreed/certainly/definitely/exactly/
> sure/true/yeah/totally/always/by all means/tell me more/
> you are right/of course/absolutely

As you read through this vocabulary, can you feel the difference these words are making in your body? Can you feel how much more open you are becoming and the energy you are now emanating? Spin the words slowly through your head and enjoy what they do to the feeling of tension and rhythm in your body. Do you feel more open now?

The accepting attitude of the YesState projects out from the body by causing it to open up the belly and chest area to an audience, moving them full on to the audience to be seen. The belly tends to lengthen, creating a taller body figure, and so increases status, yet vulnerability, to the audience. This is a confident posture. The hands become more expressive and focus around the TruthPlane, and there is a gentle smile on the face and a gentle tilt to the head to show you are listening. The whole body is more compelled to move forward to an audience, gain greater proximity and so potentially a greater level of intimacy.

Walk the Self-Talk

Here's an exercise: take a walk around a public place with your vocabulary of pure positivity swimming around in your head. Make a decision to have these "yes" words as your inner monologue. Allow your internal voice to focus only on words that have positive associations of acceptance. Start with the word "yes" and then move on to as many others as you can; then just repeat the ones you like the most over and over in your head with no effort, because you need to also pay attention to how others react to what they see. Remember, you are reciting these words silently, but notice how others look at you more, notice how others seem more drawn to you, and don't be surprised if you get stopped and asked for help. Why? Because you now have the aura of someone who can deal with things! You look as if you are open and won't rebuff or judge other human beings. You are now someone people want to go to because you accept them—this is the YesState.

Reduce Your Threat

Why is this YesState so useful? Well, it can be surprisingly easy to threaten someone's sense of status accidentally. A status threat can occur through giving advice or instructions, or simply by suggesting that someone is ineffective at a task. Many everyday conversations devolve into arguments that are driven by a status threat (the desire not to be perceived as less than another). When threatened, people may defend a position that doesn't make sense, to avoid the perceived pain of a drop in status. For example, in most people's business lives, the question, "Can I offer you some feedback?" generates an emotional response similar to that evoked by hearing the footsteps of a potential attacker behind you at night.

And the opposite of this, and power of the YesState: one scientific study showed activation of the "reward" circuitry in the brain when people were simply given positive verbal input. This occurred when participants were told, "That's correct," by a repetitive computer voice. With the YesState, you don't have to verbalize the positive vocabulary, but only to let the internal positive vocabulary infect and be reflected by your nonverbal communication, which, as we've seen, is the communication that really counts when you are creating a feeling, positive or negative. And for those who fear that they will inadvertently give their workforce too much nonverbal praise, inspiring a parade of requests for promotions and increased pay, it is widely reported that because of the deeply rewarding nature of status in and of itself, giving positive feedback may in fact reduce the perceived need for a raise in salary.

Acceptance

The YesState will help you recognize that there is absolutely no downside to projecting a physicality of total acceptance to your audience in any context. When your listeners first set eyes on you, their unconscious feeling should be, "I am wanted." From the very day we are born, the thing we really need and even crave from others (once we have been fed) is the feeling of being accepted by them. To see in their faces and in their whole body that we have a positive place with them and that we are welcome is what we desire most.

If you can give people that feeling, then you are truly perceived as an attractive human to be around, along with all that you say and stand for. Watch the Hollywood stars on the red carpet: total YesState (the open body language, gentle smile, and tilt of the head as the paparazzi fire off a hundred flashes in their face and ask a thousand crazy questions). The most gracious and starlike of them accept us, their audience, even when we invade their space in a quite brutal fashion, and we love them right back for it.

So back to the networking session: keep in the YesState, open yourself up right into your vulnerable belly area — the TruthPlane. Nod your head and give a gentle smile, opening your eyes to all the information within that assault. Take your time and you will be awed by how others come over to you — nod their heads at your points and mirror your open body language back to you, quickly moving toward your side of things.

Chapter 10 Quick Study

There may be nothing more gratifying for those individuals who are in the engineering and technology profession than the recent massive growth of the importance of technology within businesses, and so sales. Yet a common characteristic among the technical crowd is often thought to be — apart from their strong technical background—that they do not have extensive exposure to the business, the process of sales or the people skills to bridge the gaps between technology and feelings around technology.

This may be true or not, but certainly it is a pervasive stereotype that always runs the risk of playing itself out regardless of the facts or the ability of people to change their point of view, choices, or behaviors. And this puts sales and business at risk. It is the job of a great sales professional to lead the whole team in orchestrating the right sales experience for the buyer and client company. This means the sales professionals understanding their technical resources with an open mind and leading them by example in the behaviors of *Winning Body Language for Sales Professionals*, taking a coaching or mentoring role where helpful.

Just Do This Now

1. Review what you've learned so far from *Winning Body Language for Sales Professionals* and pick your number one principle, tip, or technique for winning trust with a client or customer. Now pass that tip on to the next technical resource you work with.
2. Lend your copy of this book to a technical resource you work with, pointing out the chapters you think have had the greatest effect on your performance in the sales environment.
3. Invite your technical resource out for some kind of physical activity, even if it is just for a short walk around the building to talk about strategy for the upcoming sales call. You will be surprised at the difference it makes to your relationship and trust to get physical with the people you work with.

Theory to Practice

It is easy to think of your "left-brained" technical colleagues as not wired for the "right-brained soft skills" needed to build the client relations to close sales.

But now think again. Your job is to rethink the behaviors you have seen in them and note the times when they have been soft-skilled and right-brained in a situation. Recognize the moments you have seen or heard them building relationships and building them well.

There are some functional asymmetries in the brain, and it is true that certain regions of both hemispheres are specialized for particular functions. But at the same time modern neuroscience tells us that all complex behaviors and cognitive functions require the integrated actions of multiple brain regions in both hemispheres of the brain. All types of information are likely processed in both the left and right hemispheres (perhaps in different ways, so that the processing carried out in one side of the brain complements, rather than substitutes, that being carried out in the other).

So even those technical folk who people may feel have no acumen for the right brain's relationships building in fact do have the ability *somewhere*. People just need to look for it more. And when they find it, capitalize on it.

A Body of Knowledge

Jeff Austin leads the Dynamics Services Group business unit of IndustryBuilt Software Corp. (industrybuilt.com). He comes from a long history of software implementation and excels in bridging the gap between business process and business software solutions. He believes software choice and implementation must always support the overall business and revenue goals first. Here he talks about how to build teamwork between the technical experts and sales pros.

Tech Team School

Teamwork is vital during client business meetings. As a business analyst tasked with demonstrating software to prospective clients, meetings were sometimes turned entirely over to me with only the shortest of introductions. Being left to feel my own way through the conversations often meant the clients had to repeat themselves and explain requirements that had been previously discussed. When the client began to feel comfortable with my technical ability and business knowledge, in many cases they began to address all questions to me, including those of a sales nature. Here, the sales representative struggled to retain a strong part in the conversation, and certainly wasn't guiding the meeting to his desired outcome. In these instances, we didn't work well as a team, and weren't showing ourselves to be a cohesive and cooperative unit. The client was undoubtedly left feeling that they'd met good people, but what were their thoughts about our company and our methodologies?

To promote better cooperation and teamwork between our business analysts and our sales force during meetings and demonstrations with prospective clients, we created Demo School. The goal of our Demo School was to provide the sales team with better information about our software products, techniques for more successful demonstrations, and concrete examples and real-world business scenarios. While we weren't expecting the sales team to become technical experts themselves, we did find that subsequent presentations were more inclusive, and that the sales representatives remained continuously engaged with the prospect during demos and business discussions. Better cooperation and better engagement often led to better results.

Jeremy Miller is a keynote presenter and the president of Sticky Branding (stickybranding.com). He helps companies sell more, faster, by building remarkable brands. Here he talks from his experience in the world of the hiring of sales professionals about how you can stand out nonverbally when you are selling yourself.

Interviewing for the Lizard Brain

A manager makes a decision to hire you or not within the first few moments of your interview. The rest of the meeting is spent justifying that decision.

This isn't logical. A hiring manager can't possibly hear your full story, expertise, and talents in five minutes. But her lizard brain (the brain stem) has experienced enough of you to form an opinion and inform the rest of the brain how it will decide. The process may seem rather unfair and prejudiced, but you have to deal with it and you have to prepare for it. Otherwise you're not going to get the job.

A great way to prepare for an interview is to get yourself into the "YesState." Mark Bowden taught me the technique a few years ago to help me present better on television. When you present on TV you have to convey a lot of information quickly—often in less than 90 seconds. And the YesState helped me communicate beyond my words by presenting my emotions and personality.

Thirty minutes before you go into any interview, start pushing yourself into the YesState: breathe deeply into your belly, stand up tall and square your shoulders. Look people in the eyes and smile gently. As you do these, create positive "mind chatter" or "self-talk." I often repeat the words, "Yes! Yes! Yes!" in my mind in an uplifting way. And I will tell myself that I'm here to help, I'm here to solve problems, and I'm here to listen.

I know I've achieved the right state when people come up to me and ask for directions, the time, or simply say "Hello" for no real reason. I am emoting positive energy, and my lizard brain is engaging other people's lizard brains as a "friend."

A hiring manager is taking in all that energy too at a subconscious level, and using it to determine if she likes you, wants to work with you, and thinks you'll be a good member of the team.

11

Coaching a Racehorse
Leading the Sales Team

*The man who lets a leader prescribe his course is a wreck
being towed to the scrap heap.*

—Ayn Rand

In this chapter you'll learn:

- How to create a sales environment that breeds sales champions
- To connect with your salespeople to engage and inspire
- Different communication formats for sales teams
- The nonverbal behavior of a great coach
- Physical performance for top sales leaders

Sales champions are made, not born. Obviously they have to show up for their sales career with certain aptitudes and attitudes to create an opportunity for success, but they will be turned into champions through their experiences. All great salespeople have been at some point in time transformed through their training, experiences, peer influences, and impactful managers into bankable winners. If you want to be the kind of manager who stables, trains, and owns the allegiance of those winners, you need to connect deeply with the stars and potential stars on your team. You need to dig into their habits, behaviors, attitudes, and processes to help them refine each to the sharpness of great professionals: the professionalism of champions.

Many writers and sales professionals have used sports teams as a common metaphor for sales teams, and with good reason: it is a powerful metaphor. Just like a sports team, the total result of a sales team depends on a series of individual performances by the salespeople in competition with other salespeople in the market. The quality of any individual's performance can have a major impact on whether an organization wins or loses in the market. So, while some managers may try, the reality is that the manager cannot do the work for the individual salespeople. To raise the company's odds of winning, the player has to play, and the manager has to lead and coach. The key to success is effort and resilience, but the players are judged on results, not on how hard they tried. Sales is a complete performance game, and the players and managers must find a way to win or face getting cut from the team.

Of course, you already know that the modern sales manager needs to be more like a coach than a general. You've read this from a number of sales leadership manuals already. But our guess is that you may not fully understand what that might physically mean and look like, or the positive effect on how you hit or exceed your targets that this style of leadership can have.

First, understand the nature of your players: salespeople are often independent beasts, and they have always been that way. It is a profession that demands self-reliance, self-awareness, and self-confidence. If they are any good, they are "self-starters," already revving their engines first thing in the morning (but perhaps not knowing when or where the race is really being held and how to win it)—and they're off! Often, you as the manager did not get a chance to communicate the game plan! In today's environment teams are dominated by Y-Gens—tomorrow's teams of Millennials may be even more fiercely independent! The days of the autocratic directive approach are numbered in the minuses. The *Coach* is a much stronger metaphor for the modern manager than the General of the post–World War sales demographics.

What Do You Mean, "Coach"?

Managing focuses on the completion of tasks related to work. *Coaching* is about the development of the individual to more effectively and efficiently perform those tasks. *Managers* give information and impose deadlines and objectives. *Coaches* enable individuals to find the right information, manage their own deadlines, and define their own objectives. Coaching, at its best, is a selfless act. It is about the other person, not about *you*. The coach's role is to inspire others to acquire the skills and knowledge of their craft as well as understand their own abilities in order to enable them to succeed in performing their job and developing their career. Let's pause for a moment, however, and go back to the idea of the "selfless act."

Many organizations tend to promote their top salespeople into sales management roles. While you can never say, "That will never work," it is a habit that carries considerable risk, because the skills and personal traits of top salespeople can differ starkly from the skills and attitudes of top managers/coaches. And this skill base is hard to change if it goes unacknowledged and is not provided the proper coaching and training to enable a transformation. The "pure" salesperson (independent) can learn to collaborate and work within teams—actually, the best ones usually do. But at the core of great sales performance there is usually a driving personality intent on achieving his goals, occasionally through others, but it is always his goals that are front and center. The best managers are intent on achieving goals, but these goals are most often (and for the health of the company) team goals, and the reward is seeing others flourish and the *team* win.

In their book *Discover Your Sales Strength*, Benson Smith and Tony Rutigliano describe why great managers typically say they enjoy managing:

- They enjoy developing others.
- They enjoy building a team.
- They get a kick out of helping others succeed.
- They like encouraging others to reach their objectives.
- They like working with talented people.
- They like recognizing and building what is best in other people.

The authors are saying that great managers, like great coaches, find reward in observing their impact on others. The best coaches enable others to perform so smoothly that others ultimately forget the influence of the coach. The best coaches enable members of their team to do it for themselves. This is quite different from the "reward" that might be the expected desire of a great salesperson: personal recognition and the satisfaction of winning. So when an organization promotes its star talent to management, this may not be the best move, because the behavior that created the star performer may not be the behavior needed to be a star manager/coach, and it is often rare to find individuals who have both sets of behaviors (those of star salesperson and star coach) existing simultaneously.

Organizations could pinpoint future managers in their team based on how they work with their peers and supporting resources, and not only on how much they sell. Yes, they need to be successful as salespeople, but they do not necessarily have to be the top performers. They need to be successful salespeople to understand the world of their team and share and teach sales skills to others; they just do not need to be stars.

Using Coaching to Maximize Performance

To create a great salesperson, you need to raise self-awareness and help people see their habits, behaviors, attitudes, and processes objectively. They then need to review these influences on how to manage their role on the sales team. As they go through this review, the coach and the "players" must collaborate to identify those things limiting their performance. To do this requires an open, interactive, trust-based environment, which must be built by the coach no matter what the salespeople bring to the experience.

As coach, if they are on your team, you must reach them; and if you cannot, then you either replace them or you will have to live with inconsistent progress and development. For those coaches intent on raising the bar of their team's performance, these relationships must be built; and to be consistently good at this requires you to be expert at managing your nonverbal cues to align your expression with your intentions. Done effectively, you will be able to implement a culture of continuous improvement within your teams that will lead to greatness for them and for you.

Connecting to Your Sales Team

If you are going to be a great coach, you need to be great at connecting with others because at the heart of every great coaching relationship is an intimate human relationship. The coach and the coached must connect inside an open, honest dialogue. Now, we are not talking about therapy; that is not the point at all. If the coachee needs therapy or needs to create massive change in his life, then the manager should defer to a psychologist or independent life coach.

The dialogue in a management/coaching relationship is around *performance*. It is about helping the individual see his business and career goals; helping him define an inventory of current skills and habits vital to the execution of his work responsibilities, which the individual depends upon to achieve those business and career goals. It's about helping design development strategies to enhance those skills and change any habits, all of this in order to effect an improvement in the likelihood that the individual can achieve his goals. In this case we are talking about sales performance that leads to sales goals and sales careers. At the heart of a sales coaching relationship is an intimate and honest dialogue focused on improving this performance. Done well, the relationship can be the foundation of truly phenomenal results . . . but it all starts with a *connection*.

To begin this dialogue demands that the coach invite the coachee into an open, honest environment. If this sounds like we are driving back to the recurring theme of trust and credibility . . . well, you guessed right! We are back to the GesturePlanes, and specifically the TruthPlane. Everything depends on earning that trust and credibility, and once earned, holding onto it in good times and bad.

Coaching Formats

As a sales manager, you have multiple formats available to you through which you can apply your coaching input to the team and its individuals. It's important you develop a coaching style that is adaptable when using any of these:

- Formal sales meetings
- Formal one/one meetings
- Annual performance reviews
- Ad hoc one/one meetings
- Sales appointment planning sessions
- Sales appointment debriefing sessions
- Subsets of the team—account strategy sessions
- Customer service management meetings

- Walking the floor meetings
- Informal settings: lunches/dinners/company events
- Interviewing applicants

One of the first things for every manager to remember as you look at this list, or add other situations to the list, is that you are always "on" when you lead a team. Your team members are always watching you—always! They are always assessing you. Always judging you based on your behavior. Why? Because they use their view or perception of the behavior of the tribal leader (you) to judge themselves. They mirror the leader's behavior in order to move closer to the rank or status of leader in the tribe. They mirror the leader's behavior in order to theorize how the leader sees them. And they mirror in order to fit in with other tribe (team) members.

It is therefore impossible for you to spend more time watching them than they do watching you. This is natural, as you sit higher on the organizational chart and hold a lot of influence; you have a lot of control over their job satisfaction, self-image, and fate within the organization. It also means they will see the real you no matter how much you try to cover it up. Therefore, you need to learn how to hold yourself in a posture that supports openness, honesty, and trust; and you need to form the bonds that will support a coaching relationship and an open team. We are talking about managing your nonverbal cues to ensure that they align with your intentions and support your goals of a team that pulls toward a single objective.

Formal Sales Meetings

There are many things to accomplish in a sales meeting, such as: progress toward team goals, account strategies, and perhaps win/loss discussions. In addition, one of the key components of a sales meeting is joint learning and development. This is the manager's chance to create an environment of collaboration where best practices and powerful lessons learned can be shared. At best this environment should involve a "try, make mistakes, correct, try again, and practice" model! Ideally the team should feel open enough, and trust each other enough, to be self-correcting. The team should be comfortable trying in front of their peers in role plays, making mistakes, and having their peers provide the input for correction and improvement.

Ford's Fix Everything

For my first sales management job, I was promoted from "in the team" to "lead the team." This was not a totally unexpected transition, and my fellow team members were very supportive of me in the new role. This was particularly generous of them, especially when I fell into the habit of many young managers, which is a posture that says, "Okay, now I am going to fix this place!" Of course, it is never simple to be a change catalyst, and that becomes doubly tough when as a young manager you confuse telling with teaching. I could have used the TruthPlane in those early days!

The natural posture of a young sales manager is enthusiastic excitement for change. Early in my career, I certainly took the stance of telling people what I thought should happen. After a time I came to realize that talking at people while they are standing silently by does not mean they are listening, or more important, learning. Over time I came to understand that the best sales managers are coaches, as described above.

As coaches, the challenge is to ask the questions that get the people you are managing to give answers that provide insight for them into their behavior. These questions need to be delivered in a nonjudgmental way. One of my regrets from my early sales management career is that I left the impression with some of my team members that I was judging them as wanting. Today, when coaching salespeople and sales managers, I try to focus on the person, what he is thinking, and now I ask questions that help him see how he is thinking. You cannot tell him to change; he has to be inspired to change. Once he's inspired, you can begin to collaborate with him on his development.

The techniques of Mark Bowden's *Winning Body Language* are simply wonderful tools to support these goals. They allow you to create an open, collaborative, and trust-filled environment to support a team culture of continuous improvement. Do this well and you will become a leader who people willingly follow, and the leader of a team that happily raises the bar every year.

Imagine your sales meeting: picture the room. Where does everyone sit? Do they all typically sit in the same places? What does this say to you about the hierarchy of the team, its subgroupings, and the angles and attitudes they are always taking? Is the seating distribution positive and helpful, or negative and disruptive? If it is the latter, then shake it up and put people in new places.

Now look at the seating setup. Is it a circle? Have you created a campfire? If not, think about the seating and consider how you can create that communal grouping. You might even think about changing the room setup so the team is seated in a U-shape, as a much better collaborative environment, with different team members taking the open end of the U to present from and transfer knowledge to the group.

If you feel that regular team meetings need an injection of energy, then try the "20 minute stand-up." This occurs first thing in the morning and lasts 20 minutes ONLY. No one sits. Any drinks or food cannot be put down anywhere. This leads to a dynamic that is fast-paced and energizing simply because of the environment it is set in.

To make this work, take all chairs and tables out of the meeting room that you wish to use and keep the morning refreshment outside too. As people arrive, they pick up drinks and food and enter the space. Then the meeting starts at the time designated, with the leader closing the door. The meeting finishes with the leader opening the door 20 minutes later (no matter what). Try it out and see the dynamic that unfolds when people are not sitting on some of the largest muscles in the body (the glutes), and in doing so cutting off blood circulation to some of the organs with which you are trying to communicate!

Formal One/One Meetings

The greatest opportunity for a manager to have a direct impact on the salesperson's development is inside an intimate one/one. This is a meeting that is all about helping the salesperson think through the habits, behaviors, attitudes, and processes impacting her ability to meet her goals. Done well, these meetings can form the fulcrum upon which you can raise the salesperson's performance to levels beyond anything she ever imagined before: to help her become a champion. However, none of this will happen if you cannot build an environment of trust, and that means you need to connect with her deeply, and you need to maintain that trust even when what you are learning is disquieting. It is the place where you must try not to judge, you must support.

Remember that "frequency" is an element of nonverbal communication that builds propinquity, and thus connectedness and trust. Sales managers would do well therefore to meet one-on-one with their team members at least twice a month. The foundation of this process is an orga-nized review of their on-the-job progress. This progress follows two dimen-sions: the processes they are following in the performance of their work, and their project work. These are development meetings, not performance reviews, and so the key to a successful one-on-one is for the salesperson to do most of the talking and the manager most of the listening.

The salesperson should be talking about how she is doing her work, her successes and challenges, but more important, her decision making, pri-oritizations, and progress. An effective one-on-one meeting is when the salesperson leaves with new ideas she can implement at work to improve efficiency, and the manager goes away with a clear understanding of where the salesperson stands in relation to their personal and business goals. This should all be done within a meeting that lasts as little as 30 minutes, and certainly not longer than an hour. This may sound like an ambitious goal, but if you have a framework for meetings you execute consistently, and you maintain the continuity of the bimonthly meetings, over time you will be surprised at how efficiently the meeting flows.

Before discussing how to create an efficient one-on-one meeting frame-work, let us first discuss what these meetings must not become.

They must not be interrogations: this is not a performance review meet-ing. They are not calls on the carpet: this is not your opportunity to wave the carrot and swing the stick. They cannot be all about results and what is or is not closing from the forecast. Finally, these meetings should not be regular attitude lectures or shaming events. It's not about what the sales-person is not doing, it is a meeting about *what she is* doing, *how* she is doing it, the decisions she's making that lead to these *hows*, and a discus-sion of changes that can lead to performing the work better and getting more out of the effort.

This is a meeting about her, and it is where the art of coaching truly comes to light. It is a meeting that should help raise the sales professional's self-awareness and self-confidence. It can have challenging conversations, in fact it should, but the focus should be the salesperson's thinking and decision making. The manager/coach should be pushing the salesperson to see inside her assumption, in order to bring gaps to light, or to find positives that inspire the salesperson to learn how to leverage those positives more effectively. The salesperson should leave the one-on-one, regardless of her current effectiveness, pumped, excited, and engaged to try new ideas. Done well, the salesperson should feel like the new idea was her idea; remember, coaching done well leaves the coachees thinking they did it all themselves. In other words, you do not coach for your glory, you coach for their glory.

Salesperson Operating Plans

Almost everyone talks about the value of goals and planning to salespeople, but it is often left up to them to figure out how to build their own plan. There are two immediate challenges to this approach: first, the salesperson may not have an effective framework within which to build the plan; second, every salesperson's framework and plan is unique. This uniqueness makes it opaque to the sales manager. If you are going to coach multiple salespeople at the same time, you need to have a common framework to support you looking in on their plans and providing intelligent input and support. This consistent framework creates the opportunity for efficiency and high value for both the salesperson and the manager in the one/one meetings.

Every salesperson should have his own operating plan for every year. This plan should include career goals and how he plans to move forward on those goals through this year's performance. The plan should then turn to business goals, which for a salesperson are his quota target and a variety of activity targets necessary to achieve that quota. With these objectives clearly stated, the salesperson needs to turn to the projects and tasks he needs to complete to achieve those activity and quota targets. Finally, he should then categorize the tasks, in order to allocate his daily, weekly, and monthly time appropriately. This last element is the time management principle of "Time Blocking."

Time Blocking

The most valuable asset a salesperson has is time, and the best salespeople know how to leverage this asset to increase the chances they have for success. Stephen Covey in his classic book *Seven Habits of Highly Effective People* draws up a two-by-two grid of urgency and importance. The grid places every task a person performs within a range from "Urgent and Important" to "Not Urgent and Not Important." When people then note their daily time allocations, they usually find that most of their time is in the urgent quadrants of Important or Not Important.

Urgent and Important	Not Urgent, Important
Urgent, Not Important	Not Urgent and Not Important

The challenge with this classification is that for most people the highest value and greatest long-term performance leverage comes from time in the "Not Urgent, Important" quadrant. The purpose of categorizing tasks is to be able to designate which are in this important but not urgent quadrant.

Now, as the salesperson looks at her weekly and monthly plan, she can assign time blocks, either two or four hours long, for each of these nonurgent but important high-leverage tasks that lead to the greatest future performance. It then becomes this information that is brought into the one-on-one meetings for the salesperson to review, and then have the manager/coach guide the salesperson's decision making to ensure that these tasks get done too. In this way, the coaching will evolve into helping the salesperson see how the habits and behaviors in her priorities and in her work impact her performance. Then the two can collaborate around how to make changes to these habits and behaviors to improve how she does her work, and ultimately the results.

Using the salesperson's operating plan, it becomes possible in the one-on-one meeting to review what is actually happening in the salesperson's weeks versus the original time block plan. It is relatively easy to now see what is not being done according to the plan and to discuss what is creating the gap. What decisions is the salesperson making in the flow of her work related to priorities that create the gap? For example, is her e-mail always on? Does she treat every e-mail as urgent? Does she carry her mobile phone with her and check it every two minutes? Did her plan call for this level of e-mail priority, or is it a convenient distraction from the real work she's trying to get done?

This is an easy and obvious example, but it is amazing how true it is. Other examples include the misappropriation of urgency around prospecting or cold calling.

Cold Calling/Prospecting: Important but Never Urgent

Ask yourself the following question: "What would make you cancel an appointment at the last minute with a prospect or customer?" The answer to this question usually relates to something pretty calamitous:

death in the family, terrible accident, etc. In other words most salespeople will drag themselves over broken glass to make an appointment with a prospect or customer.

Now ask yourself: "What has to happen for you to cancel an appointment you made in your calendar to yourself to make your cold calls?" And your answer to this question is most likely driven by urgency and not importance. Some readers will be saying, "Well if a customer calls and needs something, or there is an emergency in my e-mail." Most will admit that virtually anything of even the most modest urgency is sufficient to get them out of that cold calling appointment.

For a moment let's look at this decision-making process that bumps prospecting so easily. Let's talk about the apparent legitimacy of the customer call.

On first blush this seems like a reasonable answer; however, let's look at it a little deeper. If you, as a salesperson, were on your way to an appointment with a customer and another customer called with a problem, would you cancel the first customer appointment? More significantly, if you were in the appointment with the customer or prospect and the customer with a problem called, what would happen? Well, the problem call would likely go to your voice mail, and it would sit there until you finished the appointment. So, why is it different when you are making cold calls?

The difference is it feels more urgent, and maybe it is, but it is probably not more *important*—at least not in the context of your goals. Prospecting is probably just as important a step in achieving your sales goals as dealing with customer service issues, maybe even more important. The point is that whether it is an e-mail, last minute customer service issues, or any other distraction, the salesperson is letting the urgent overwhelm the important. And of course this is classic reptilian brain thinking: *now is always more important than the future.* But by using the operating plan and a regular review in a calm and social environment (not the interrogation-cell atmosphere of the "come to Jesus meeting") of where time went, the manager/coach can engage the neocortex of the sales professional and help her see how the decision making around priorities is limiting her performance.

Loosening the Screws

Imagine your one-on-one environment, which is probably your office. Consider for a moment that most salespeople are nervous in a one-on-one. This nervousness often comes from a fear of being judged and found wanting. Remember we said that one-on-ones are developmental? The goal of a sales manager/coach is to relax the salesperson and to get her to look objectively at how she is working in relation to her plan. The goal is not to spark reptilian brains into fight-or-flight with you. This means you must create an environment of collaboration, and you must position yourself to focus on the salesperson in a nonconfrontational way.

If something is being done incorrectly, or if the salesperson is missing something in her habits, behaviors, attitude, or processes, then the goal is to get her to see it. In other words the posture has to always inspire her to do the talking, which means you ask questions that push the salesperson to the right realizations, ultimately forcing her to do most of the talking.

This is hard for many managers, and the natural inclination is to lean on the "tell" model of management. To resist this urge and keep the mood right for open collaboration and an objective assessment of what is being done and what needs to be done, you should first think about all the TV shows, films, or documentaries you have seen where someone gets interrogated. Think about the way the room is set up—the furniture, lighting, and the orientation of the seating. How are the subjects for interrogation brought into the room? Even when the interrogator is being the "nice guy," what is it about the situation that alerts you to the aggression and hostility?

Now think about the body language of the interrogator. How does he sit, stand, walk, question, and listen? Of course as a manager you are always a chief of intelligence. And to this end when gathering intelligence in a meeting, you must adopt an attitude that is expectant of that data in order to compliment the person opening up to you. But at the same time it is so easy when under pressure and stress to fall into the attitude and posturing of an interrogator or inquisitor—which often only causes your "subject" to make up data in order to please you and stop the aggression or shut down the channel of correct data in order to protect herself from any punishments that might arise from giving you "bad news." Let' s look at some of the body language of a caricatured interrogator that you may have imagined yourself, in order to first know what we must *not* do.

Torment

Imagine your team member sitting in a low chair a short distance opposite you, across a table. He is "parked" entirely in hunched-up shoulders almost meeting his ears, hands protectively placed in the lap. His whole body is hunched over as you stand, looming above him from across your desk, your hands pressed down on it, your chest broad and puffed out, pushing its way into his personal space. Your chin is tucked in, your forehead down, and your eye contact is strong, yet he very rarely looks at you. Most of the time he looks down or away. In order to make your points clearly, you point at him and jab your finger toward his eyes in a staccato manner.

Advocate

Alternatively, we have the trustworthy body language of a coaching leader: you sit at a 90-degree angle to your team member at the end of a table and at the same height in your chair as him. You are relaxed yet alert—fully present. At the corner of the table between you there are perhaps snacks that you are sharing, and drinks. You sit at enough distance from the table to be more visible and open to him, yet not so far that you exit his personal space. You are being sure to allow your team member to do most of the talking, and you are doing most of the listening. Every now and then you ask a question with your hands open in the TruthPlane. As your team member responds with his experience and opinions, your head is tilted to one side and you gently smile and nod, especially when he opens up with more data for you.

You can obviously appreciate the difference in experience and openness here in contrast to the interrogation cell scenario. But sometimes you need to give your opinion and assert some authority. What then?

I Am the Law!

Sales appointment planning sessions, sales appointment debriefing sessions, account strategy sessions, and performance reviews are developmental, but they are also a time when it is appropriate to judge and assess the salesperson with an eye to directed focus toward the next year's improvements. The results of these sessions and reviews should then be incorporated into the candidate's operating plans for the next year. You are still guiding and collaborating, but you are the boss in this meeting more than the friend.

Think about bringing yourself a few inches in front of the DoorPlane to achieve the calm, assertive, nonverbal communication that comes with the gesturing in the TruthPlane that you should already be doing, but adding the extra edge of dominance to your body language that asserts you as an "alpha" character in the room.

As the sales manager, your team will look to you for guidance to support their sales success. The keyword is "guidance." The developmental goal is to support the salesperson or team learning how to build successful sales strategies and tactics. As sales manager, early in your relationship you may be doing most of the designing, but your goal is to have the person or team develop so that they can contribute more and more of their plans and assessments.

To create this environment, again imagine a meeting setting in your office, let's say it is a small meeting room. There are two of you, and you are looking at a whiteboard and have your laptops open for quick research. Both of you should sit initially, and then one of you goes to the whiteboard to take some notes. If possible, make this the salesperson. When she stands, she will feel like she is in control of the meeting. Now from your seated position, help her lead the discussion. Push back your chair and swivel to face her at the whiteboard. Show you are open to her ideas and opinions by having your hands in the TruthPlane. As she brings forward points, nod gently and smile and find opportunities to write down some of the ideas into your personal notes, clearly verbalizing that the suggestion is a good one. Then you add your suggestions on top.

Walking the Floor Meetings

When a sales manager walks into the sales bullpen, what happens? Does everyone sit up straighter; is everyone just a little on edge? If so, this says the sales manager is an intruder, not a member of the bullpen. Collaboration calls for the sales manager to be a part of the team, leading the team for sure, but more important, leading the team's collaboration. The sales manager on the floor should be welcomed and engaging, and as such should manage his posture to be welcoming and engaging. Here are some ways to behave that display your openness to the team in a number of scenarios.

Informal Settings: Lunches, Dinners, Company Events

Let your hair down. In these environments the goal is to let the team relax and bond. It is an opportunity for the sales manager to facilitate the conversation, but not dominate it. This is the place to help the team get to know each other and build trust. The role in this instance is as patriarch/matriarch, but in an empowering way. There should be no question who the leader is, but the leader should be focused on creating an environment where team members feel comfortable sharing a little of themselves.

Imagine a dinner table, and you as manager and six of your team members sitting down to dinner. Naturally you will sit at the head of the table, and from that position you will orchestrate the event. What you want to do next is help the team members to do the talking and to express themselves. You also want to build up each speaker, give each your full attention, and help that person feel important to promote an atmosphere of shared respect and support.

A great practice is to arrange with a team member beforehand to swap places with you at dessert. The benefits: she gets the head of the table and a feeling of raise in rank, and you get closer proximity to any members who have had a greater distance from you for most of the meal. Everyone feels special, and status is evened out a little as you move toward the close of the event.

Sales Calls with Prospects and Customers

This is one of the hardest developmental environments for sales managers, because it feels like there is so much at stake, that is, a sales opportunity. Most managers struggle to let the salesperson run the sales call without interfering. They should resist this if they can. You see, the goal is to create independent salespeople who can go and sell to multiple customers without your assistance. This is how you expand your reach, increase your coverage, and grow your business. This goal is the higher goal, and not stepping in, or over, your salesperson in a call because you would like to do it differently. As mentioned, this is very hard to do, and will really test your mettle as a sales manager. Can you sit by and watch someone do something differently from you and leave it alone?

If in the end you must step in, then you need to make sure you do not discredit the salesperson's authority completely when you do it. The goal is to have the salesperson continue to manage this opportunity after the meeting, so you cannot afford to make her look bad, as it will hamper her ability to lead the sale after you leave. To do this means using the techniques in

Winning Body Language to manage yourself and remain calm and assertive throughout, making sure to keep everyone's status up in the room. This is the behavior of a great leader rather than an ego-starved tyrant.

Chapter 11 Quick Study

Top performers have great leaders to guide them to reaching their potential. And this is the same for top-performing teams too. Those great leaders, like any top-performing sales professional, are great listeners rather than "tellers" when it really counts. They are able to then understand where a potential sales star is in relation to his goals, and to guide that person by either imparting experience or training or telling simple stories to help him on his way, and, most important, to ask him what he is going to do today to reach those goals. This requires the body language of a coach: calm and assertive, and open when listening.

Do This Now

Having read this chapter,

1. What do *you* think you should do now in order to maximize your nonverbal performance as a sales manager in order to increase the performance of your team overall?

    _____

2. What else should you do today?

    _____

3. And what else?

    _____

Theory to Practice

Who in your work life has bought out the best performance in you? When they were instructing, coaching, mentoring, or advising you, how did their body language help them get through to you? Remember what they were doing that made you feel recognized, appreciated, and able to take on the value they had to bring to developing you to a fuller potential.

Now how can you mirror their behavior for others and discover what it does for them too?

A Body of Knowledge

Karen Wright is an executive coach and the owner of Parachute Executive Coaching (parachuteexecutivecoaching.com). She and her team provide executive and leadership coaching services to support the development of current and emerging leaders in organizations. She is the author of *The Complete Executive—The 10-Step System for Powering Up Peak Executive Performance*. Here she talks about what to physically dial up and dial down as a sales team leader.

Big in Sales

When I'm asked to work with a client, I get briefed on their situation—their strengths and their challenges. The typical sales team leader is often described as brilliant with customers but "rough around the edges" in their interactions with internal colleagues, direct reports, and support staff. When I probe for details, I usually hear "bull in a china shop" or "doesn't listen" or "is in everyone's face." Unfortunately, when very talented salespeople deliver consistently and get promoted, they're put into a position of leading people but having very little direct contact with the customer, and their best tricks and tactics don't work anymore—quite the opposite, in fact. Sales leaders tend to be "big" personalities. They're extroverted and exuberant and the life of the party, perfect for magnetically attracting customers and creating a powerful network. When they become a leader of people, however, they need to dial down their need for the spotlight in favor of letting their team members shine.

Best suggestions for a sales superstar to make the transition to leader successfully are all about being more approachable and less dominant. Try adopting more open body language—eye contact, relaxed posture, measured pace of speaking. Use the listening skills that helped you so well with customers. Let silence be your teaching tool—don't leap to fill space when coaching your team members. Spend time building relationships with service providers and support staff—pay attention to their stories and observe their work space to notice the things that are important to them. Trust that you don't need to solve or deliver, at least not directly—and that by letting others fill the space, you'll be creating the necessary capacity around you.

A Concluding Thought

Can't learn it in an office, gotta learn it in the street.
And you sure can't buy it, you gotta live it.
—Shelly, *Glengarry Glen Ross*, David Mamet

My first sales job was at the age of 16 in a gas station: fuel, oil, windshield wash, and automobile air fresheners—that stuff could sell itself.

In my time off I had another sales job going door-to-door hawking TV satellite dishes. At the time there were no broadcasts of the actual content as yet—just the hardware. It was a tricky sell, to say the least. I was not downhearted. The company collapsed within a month, which saved me from the dishonor of throwing in the towel.

So I got myself another sales job in a high-street men's clothing store where I was taught my first piece of really great sales technique, and which has stuck with me ever since:

The manager came up to me one day, after hearing me crash and burn trying to talk a customer into buying, and said, "Mark, let me give you some advice. *Get the jacket on their back.* Once you have the jacket on the gentleman's back, then the suit is as good as sold."

And from that point on all I would do is watch customers to see which line of jackets they would touch. I would move gently alongside and pull out the jacket in their fit (you got an eye for sizing that up), deftly pull it from its hanger and hold it up and open it for them with a little flourish. "Try it on," I'd say, firmly. They would. I would brush down on their shoulders and then move around to the front to button up the jacket and straighten the lapels—like a parent on the first day of "big school." Then move out of their way so they could see themselves in the full-length mirror ahead of them, as I smiled proudly at how they now looked.

They would often leave with not one but sometimes two or even three suits.

There is no doubt in my mind to this day that selling is a physical thing. It is a *feeling* that sells the merchandise. So no matter what you are selling,

"Get the jacket on their back."

Mark Bowden
truthplane.com

Appendix

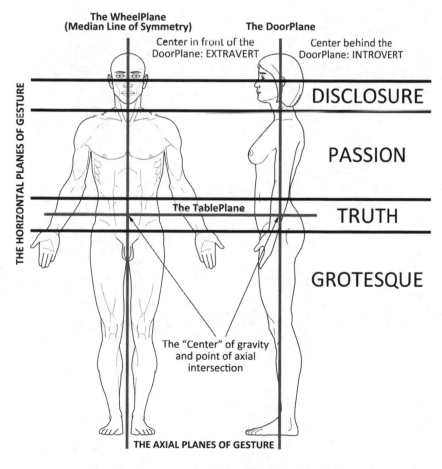

Figure A-1   GesturePlane System for Sales Professionals

Further Reading and Resources

A list of books and articles referred to, consulted, or of related interest.

Ardrey, Robert, and Berdine Ardrey. *The Territorial Imperative: A Personal Inquiry into the Animal Origins of Property and Nations.* Atheneum, 1966.

Bandler, Richard, and John Grinder. *The Structure of Magic* (2 vols). Science and Behavior Books, 1976.

Bandler, Richard, and John La Valle. *Persuasion Engineering.* Meta Publications, 1996.

Barrett, Louise. *Beyond the Brain — How Body and Environment Shape Animal and Human Minds.* Princeton University Press, 2011.

Bickerton, Derek. *Adam's Tongue — How Humans Made Language, and Language Made Humans.* Hill and Wang, 2010.

Bosworth, Michael. *Solution Selling: Creating Buyers in Difficult Selling Markets.* McGraw-Hill, 1994.

Bowden, Mark. *Winning Body Language: Control the Conversation, Command Attention, and Convey the Right Message — Without Saying a Word.* McGraw-Hill, 2010.

Bradner, Erin, and Gloria Mark. *Why Distance Matters: Effects on Cooperation, Persuasion and Deception.* Dept. of Information and Computer Science, University of California, 2002.

Brafman, Ori, and Rom Brafman. *Click: The Forces Behind How We Fully Engage with People, Work, and Everything We Do.* Crown Business, 2011.

Carnegie, Dale. *How to Win Friends and Influence People.* Simon & Schuster, 1934.

Carter, Rita. *Mapping the Mind.* University of California Press, 2000.

Chartrand, Tanya L., and John A. Bargh. "The Chameleon Effect: The Perception–Behavior Link and Social Interaction," *Journal of Personality and Social Psychology*, 76 (1999), 6, 893–910.

Cialdini, Robert. *Influence: Science and Practice.* Pearson, 2009.

Cook, Ian A., et al., "Regional Brain Activation with Advertising Images," *Journal of Neuroscience, Psychology, and Economics*, 4 (2011): 3.

Covey, Stephen. *Seven Habits of Highly Effective People.* Free Press, 2004.Coyle, Daniel. *The Talent Code: Greatness Isn't Born, It's Grown, Here's How.* Bantam, 2009.

Crowley, Amado, "The Neophyte Robe by Master Amado 777," http://amado-crowley.net, 1999.

Damasio, Antonio. *Descartes' Error: Emotion, Reason, and the Human Brain.* Penguin, 2005.

Darwin, Charles. *On the Origin of Species by Means of Natural Selection, or the Preservation of Favoured Races in the Struggle for Life.* John Murray, 1859.

Darwin, Charles. *Works of Charles Darwin: Including On the Origin of Species, The Descent of Man, The Expression of Emotions in Man and Animals.* MobileReference Kindle Edition, 2000.

Dawkins, Richard. *The Selfish Gene.* Oxford University Press, 1989.

Dixon, Matt, and Brent Adamson. *The Challenger Sale: Taking Control of the Customer Conversation.* Portfolio Hardcover, 2011.

Eibl-Eibesfeldt, Irenäus. *Human Ethology (Foundations of Human Behavior).* Aldine Transaction, 2007.

Ekman, Paul. *Emotions Revealed: Recognizing Faces and Feelings to Improve Communication and Emotional Life*. Holt, 2007.

Ekman, Paul, and Karl G. Heider, "The Universality of Contempt Expression: A Replication," *Motivation and Emotion*, 12 (1998): 303–308.

Hogan, Robert, "Hogan Assessments," http://www.hogan assessments.com.

Holmes, Hannah. *The Well-Dressed Ape: A Natural History of Myself*. Random House, 2009.

Jung, Carl. *Psychological Types* (The Collected Works of C. G. Jung, vol. 6). Princeton University Press, 1976.

Kahan, Dan M., Hank Jenkins-Smith, and Donald Braman, "Cultural Cognition of Scientific Consensus," *Journal of Risk Research*, 14 (2011), 147–174.

Lecoq, Jacques. *The Moving Body: Teaching Creative Theatre*. Routledge, 2001.

Lecoq, Jacques, and David Bradby. *Theatre of Movement and Gesture*. Routledge, 2006.

Ledo, Joseph. *The Emotional Brain: The Mysterious Underpinnings of Emotional Life*. Simon & Schuster, 1998.

Lee, Kang, et al., "Children's Use of Triadic Eye Gaze: Information for "Mind Reading," *Developmental Psychology*, 34 (1998), 3, 525–539.

Lewis, Thomas, Fari Amini, and Richard Lannon. *A General Theory of Love*. Vintage, 2001

Logan, Dave, John King, and Halee Fischer-Wright. *Tribal Leadership: Leveraging Natural Groups to Build a Thriving Organization*. Harper-Business, 2008.

Mehrabian, Albert, and Susan R. Ferris, "Inference of Attitudes from Nonverbal Communication in Two Channels," *Journal of Consulting Psychology*, 31(3), 1967.

Mehrabian, Albert, and Morton Wiener, "Decoding of Inconsistent Communications," *Journal of Personality and Social Psychology*, 6(1), 1967.

Mirodan, Vladimir, "The Way of Transformation: The Laban-Malmgren System of Dramatic Character Analysis," PhD thesis, University of London, 1997.

Rock, David, "SCARF: A Brain-Based Model for Collaborating with and Influencing Others," *NeuroLeadership Journal*, 1, 2008.

Rosen, Keith. *Coaching Salespeople into Sales Champions: A Tactical Playbook for Managers and Executives.* Wiley, 2008

Ryan, Christopher, and Cacilda Jethá. *Sex at Dawn: The Prehistoric Origins of Modern Sexuality.* Harper, 2010.

Simons, Herbert. *The Sciences of the Artificial.* MIT Press, 1996.

Smith, Benson, and Tony Rutigliano. *Discover Your Sales Strengths: How the World's Greatest Salespeople Develop Winning Careers.* Business Plus, 2003.

Stringer, Chris, and Peter Andrews. *The Complete World of Human Evolution.* Thames & Hudson, 2012.

Index

About the Authors

Mark Bowden received his university degree in performance in the United Kingdom and studied the gesture control methods of Jacques Lecoq's Laboratory of Movement in Paris. He worked with some of the world's groundbreaking theater companies, appearing in multi-award-winning stage and screen productions globally and training internationally recognized actors and directors. Mark went on to work with leading practitioners of movement psychology and built upon the influence techniques of Dr. Milton Erickson.

Mark is the creator of TruthPlane™, a communication training company and a unique methodology for anyone who has to communicate to an audience. His communication techniques, which he trains to individuals and groups worldwide, are used by top executives and political leaders around the globe who want to gain an advantage beyond words when they speak. Over his 20 years of experience, he has garnered a reputation for being one of the world's expert performance trainers and is highly sought after for his business presentation skills at such universities as international top 10 business school Schulich at York University, Rotman School of Business in Toronto, and McGill in Montreal. His client list of leading businesspeople, teams, and politicians currently includes presidents and CEOs of Fortune 500 companies and prime ministers of G8 countries.

He gives highly entertaining and informative keynote speeches on persuasive and influential verbal and nonverbal language and communication structures that help you stand out, win trust, and profit every time you speak. His bestselling body language book, *Winning Body Language*, has been translated into five languages.

Mark can be contacted via www.TruthPlane.com.

Andrew Ford is a sales performance management consultant, trainer, and coach. As founder of Sales CoPilot, with clients across North America, he has a proven track record of success at building high-performing sales teams with increased retention, improved efficiency, and better closing ratios. He specializes in three types of projects: sales model transformations, rapid sales team scaling to capture markets, and sales performance improvement to smooth out lumpy sales results. His objective in all projects is to improve the efficiencies of every aspect of the sales organization to increase sales funnel through-put to help clients sell more and sell faster.

Andrew can be found via www.SalesCoPilot.com.